PIONEERS
IN
MARKETING

A collection of twenty-five biographies
of men who contributed to the growth of
marketing thought and action.

Edited by
John S. Wright
and
Parks B. Dimsdale, Jr.

Publishing Services Division
School of Business Administration
Georgia State University
Atlanta, Georgia

1974

Published by the Publishing Services Division
School of Business Administration,
Georgia State University, 33 Gilmer St. S.E.,
Atlanta, Ga. 30303

Cover design by Fredd Chrestman.

Contents

Preface

Marketing has only recently become established as a recognized discipline within the education for business environment. The comparative newness of marketing thought is illustrated by the fact that its pioneers were born in the 1870s and 1880s and their contributions came in the 1930s, 1940s, and the 1950s. Some of the long-lived still contribute useful insights. Present-day students and practitioners of marketing, however, know very little about the architects of the marketing discipline. The goal of this volume is to help remedy this situation - to fill the void.

By the mid-1950s, marketing had progressed beyond the formative stage. Its professional organization, the American Marketing Association, had been in existence for a couple of decades and affirmative steps were being taken to enhance the stature of the discipline.

One step was to recognize marketing's early leaders. To this end, the AMA established a Committee on Biographies with Perry Bliss serving as Chairman. Other Committee members included Wroe Alderson, Albert W. Frey, E. T. Grether, John E. Jeuck, Fred M. Jones, and Franklin Lynip. The purpose of the group was set down in the *Journal of Marketing* in these words:

"In order to pay tribute to the men who have been leaders in the field of marketing, some years ago the American Marketing Association established a Committee on Biographies to run a series of statements on the pioneers in the field. In this series the Association honors the distinguished men of the past, and those of the present who are approaching retirement, who have contributed in an outstanding way to the thought and development of marketing."

The work of the Committee on Biographies culminated in a *Pioneers in Marketing* series which commenced with the publication of a biographical sketch concerning Professor Roland Snow Vaile in the April, 1956 issue of the *Journal of Marketing*. A total of 23 pioneers were highlighted between that date and October, 1961 when the last sketch appeared. (The series was superseded by the *Leaders in Marketing* profiles which have been published regularly since then. This series is scheduled for termination in January, 1974).

Twelve of the men featured were deceased at the time their biographies appeared in the *Journal*; these sketches are reprinted as originally published. For the eleven persons who died following the time they were featured or were living as we gathered materials for this book, an effort was made to update information about their contributions to marketing. Letters were directed to the person who wrote the original sketch, or in some cases to the person himself or someone who might know of his career pattern after publication of the sketch. Seven of the biographies now carry an "afternote" wherein new information is provided. Professor Duncan made extensive changes in the sketch dealing with Paul Nystrom. Because the original writer requested that his sketches on Ralph Starr Butler and Stanley B. Resor not be reprinted, we asked Professors J. Howard Westing and Laurence Wile Jacobs to do completely new biographies on those two men. No information could be found concerning the post-publication activities of one person.

As a "bonus" biography, Professor Persis Emmett Rockwood has contributed a completely new sketch about Clarence Saunders. Although Mr. Saunders did not appear in the original collection of pioneers, surely his activities warranted inclusion if the series had been prolonged. Reavis Cox similarly wrote an extra sketch about his Wharton School colleague, Ralph F. Breyer.

These priceless biographies are brought together in this volume with the kind permission of the American Marketing Association. The editors hope that scholars and businessmen alike will find these sketches interesting. Marketing owes a great deal to the twenty-four men featured here. They have laid a solid foundation, both in theory and in practice. Their work provides a challenge to those of us currently treading the marketing trail.

John S. Wright
Parks B. Dimsdale, Jr.

Atlanta
January 1974

Hugh Elmer Agnew
1875-1955

1

Hugh Elmer Agnew
1875-1955

by WILLIAM J. McKEON

HUGH ELMER AGNEW was born in Hillsdale County, Michigan, January 31, 1875. Exactly eighty years later he died, July 31, 1955, after a long and distinguished service to marketing and business.

His entry on the academic scene took place as Superintendent of Schools, Portland, Michigan (1898-1901), after graduation from State Normal College, Ypsilanti, Michigan. He continued his academic work and received a degree from University of Michigan in 1902. After a year as Superintendent of Schools at Howell, Michigan, he moved into the fields of business and publishing. For a decade he published a newspaper in Dowagiac, Michigan, and found time also to conduct a profitable mail order business in printing.

With this background, Dr. Agnew joined the Journalism Department at the University of Washington, where he nurtured a single course in Marketing into a series of courses (1913-1916), out of which grew the School of Commerce at that University, the first evidence of his pioneering proclivities in marketing.

In 1916 Dr. Agnew was back in the business field for two years as Sales Manager of A. Schilling and Company, and then back to journalism as Editor of *Western Advertising* and the *Automotive News*. His challenging approach in the editorial columns of these publications developed controversy that stimulated specific advances in thought in both these fields. In 1920 he moved to the editorial staff of *Printers' Ink* and became a frequent contributor to to *Printers' Ink Monthly*.

In 1920, too, he joined the Department of Marketing faculty of New York University as Associate Professor and attained the rank of Professor in 1922. He became Chairman of the Department in

Journal of Marketing
Vol. XXIV No. 3, January, 1960
Reprinted by Permission

1928 and continued in that post until his retirement. Here his influence was manifest in the realignment of the Marketing curriculum to integrate and broaden the coverage and give due recognition to areas outside the direct fields of advertising and selling. Under his guidance Marketing Research areas of the curriculum were given added stimulus.

By 1926 Dr. Agnew's journalistic efforts began to take book format, and by 1941 he had authored or co-authored some half dozen books in diverse fields of advertising and general marketing and extensive articles for the *Encyclopaedia Britannica.* His *Cooperative Advertising by Competitors* (1926), *Advertising Media—How to Weigh and Measure* (1932), *Outdoor Advertising* (1938) and *Marketing Policies* (1941) are considered pioneering works in their respective fields. Even when read against the developments of a generation, some of these contributions still seem timely. He also co-authored the widely used text, *Outlines of Marketing,* through three editions (1936, 1942, 1950).

His early efforts at measurement in the field of advertising media made him a recognized force in the drive which still continues, to attempt to demonstrate the value received for the huge investments being made in advertising space and time. His book on the subject was merely a jumping-off point. His speeches before advertising and media groups stimulated critical discussion which moved the goal discernibly nearer. Without the benefit of present-day measurement techniques, he offered some stimulating and meaningful observations in the area.

His *Marketing Policies* literally pioneered the currently popular area of Marketing Management. Approaching marketing from a qualitative rather than a quantitative angle, it viewed marketing aspects from the standpoint of "What is it worth?" rather than "What is it or where did it come from?" The volume also presented for the first time significant treatment of such topics as leased departments of stores and supermarkets, interstate barriers to trade, and sampling.

In the affairs of the American Marketing Association, Dr. Agnew was an equally progressive factor. In 1915 he was a participant at the first meeting of a group that has since grown into the AMA. This group, which formally organized at the meeting, named itself the National Association of Teachers of Advertising. The name, interestingly enough, was fully descriptive of the interests of a large majority of the members, since the teaching of marketing at that early date had not yet emerged as of great importance. Through the name changes that marked the growing importance of marketing in both the Association and the business world, Dr. Agnew maintained a constant and active interest in the Association, serving it in numerous capacities, including Secretary (1929-1935) and President (1936). It was his responsibility, as well as his reward for a long-time campaign, to close the affairs of the old Association and to pass on the gavel to Frank R. Coutant, first president of the American Marketing Association in 1937.

In a short history of the Association prepared by Dr. Agnew for the 25th Anniversary Dinner of the Association and printed in the *JOURNAL OF MARKETING* (April, 1941), Dr. Agnew summed up his sketch of the Association's development by again flinging down the gauntlet to both teachers and businessmen when he wrote: "We have passed the place where we teach only what business does. We do not hesitate to criticize business where it is inefficient in method or uneconomic in purpose."

Today this is hardly a challenge; rather it is a fact. But eighteen years have seen much change. At that time, it is true, the leaders in the field practiced Dr. Agnew's dogma, but many a teacher and practitioner did not.

In addition to his other extracurricular activities, Dr. Agnew's contributions to advertising were particularly important during the period 1922-1925 when he served as Director of Research for the Periodical Publishers Association. During this time he issued about one hundred studies of the leading advertisers in various fields, as well as related material.

Another of his contributions to the evaluation of advertising media was a major study involving some 22,000 New York City families, to determine newspaper reading habits in that city. The critical analysis of the research findings opened a fresh avenue of evaluation for the researchers of the day.

During the 1930s Dr. Agnew was of much value to business as a marketing consultant and expert witness in business litigation. Among others he served the Bulova Watch Co., National Distillers Products Co. vs. K. Taylor Distilling Co., and Standard Brands.

In 1935 Dr. Agnew received the honorary degree of Litt.D. from Huntington College, Huntington, Indiana, and in 1942 the honorary degree of LL.D. from Hillsdale College, Hillsdale, Michigan.

Perhaps a single observation cannot be made to sum up Dr. Agnew's contributions. Many of them are not of a formal nature. But his stimulating mind spurred many others to extend themselves in their work. The single characteristic that seemed most outstanding was a soundness of judgment which he applied to any problem before him.

Ralph F. Breyer
1897-

2

Ralph F. Breyer
1897-

by REAVIS COX

Ralph F. Breyer belongs to a generation younger than the one to which we usually refer when we speak of the "pioneers" of marketing. These "pioneers" are the men who, late in the nineteenth or early in the twentieth century, began to teach marketing under one name or another and to develop marketing research as a consulting profession. Their first books on various aspects of marketing appeared before the great depression of 1929-1933. Breyer began teaching in that period; but his main works were published between 1931 and 1949.

He nevertheless must be called a "pioneer" because, from the outset, he placed emphasis both upon assembling information not previously known to systematic students of marketing and upon developing new concepts of the nature and functioning of marketing. As the years went on he began to put increasing emphasis on the second task. He merits designation as a "leader" because his work with what he came to call "the marketing institution" helped prepare the way for a recent burgeoning of efforts both to understand and to manage channels of distribution. He also contributed to the working out of techniques for measuring distribution costs (what some students prefer to call value added by distribution) and for helping managements relate what they spend for marketing activities to the revenue these activities produce. Like many another innovator, he had difficulty in getting a hearing for what he had to say; but he has lived long enough to see the seeds he planted begin to bear fruit.

This sketch was especially written for this volume. Dr. Breyer was not featured in the "Pioneers in Marketing" series.

9

As the son of a Baltimore grocer, he was born into marketing in 1897. He completed the first two years of his undergraduate work at Franklin and Marshall College. He then entered the Army in World War I, and when he was discharged he transferred to the Wharton School. His career there began in the fall of 1920, when he became an instructor in Commerce and Transportation. It closed in 1968, when he retired and was appointed Emeritus Professor of Marketing. In the interval he advanced through the academic ranks from instructor to full professor, meanwhile receiving his M.A. in 1923 and his Ph.D. in 1925. His first book was his doctoral dissertation, published in 1925 under the title *Agents and Contracts in Export Trade*. Since 1968 he has lived in quiet retirement in Florida.

Breyer's natural bent was for scholarly work based on extensive and intensive reading, prolonged meditation, and thoroughly planned teaching. It was well served by the environment into which he settled; but misfortune soon intervened to deprive him of its full benefits, when he suddenly and completely lost his hearing. Hearing devices gave him no help. So for more than three decades he had to work in the isolation that total deafness inflicts. He read enormously, reflected uninterruptedly, and continued his teaching, for which he devised viable routines. But he could no longer engage in detailed conversations and interviews nor benefit from informal discussions, committee meetings, conferences, and lectures.

His first major book, developed as reading assignments for one of his classes, appeared in 1931 under the title *Commodity Marketing*. This was one of a very few textbooks outside of agricultural marketing that undertook to teach general marketing by making a detailed survey of the marketing system used for each of a number of commodities, or more properly, industries. Since materials on farm products were becoming plentiful, he limited his field to some fourteen non-agricultural commodities and two services --- electricity and telephones.

The book is a strong one of its kind. In writing it, Breyer strengthened his great capacity for the patient, painstaking and laborious assembly of facts from many scattered sources and their organization into systematic descriptions. However, the method used left unsatisfied what he himself has called his "natural aptitude for seeking the wholeness and order in marketing phenomena, and other phenomena for that matter." For his next major work he therefore shifted to what he called the institutional approach to marketing and published, in 1934, *The Marketing Institution*.

In his use of the term *institutional*, Breyer combined into *one* concept what most other writers have divided into two. What they called the institutional approach concentrates its attention upon describing the agencies of marketing. It finds these by observation, then classifies and counts them. In due course it emerges with voluminous descriptive statistics best exemplified in the massive reports of the *Census of Business*. The functional approach, in contrast, concentrates attention upon what the marketing agencies do. Breyer felt that the two approaches could not logically be separated because agencies can usefully be classified and subjected to analysis only on the basis of what they do.

The first three parts of *The Marketing Institution* are one of the classics of marketing literature. (Part IV is a perceptive but now outdated evaluation of the effects of Roosevelt's New Deal legislation upon marketing.) Since the original is itself highly condensed, it is not easily summarized. Suffice it to say that in some 250 pages, Breyer offers statements that have never been surpassed for penetration and incisiveness on the tasks performed by marketing as an economic institution; the nature and structure of the marketing machinery that does the work; the significance of the marketing setting for what goes on; how supply and demand work in the marketing system; the flow, action and interaction of marketing forces; the significance of time and space for marketing, types of competition and their intensity; the cost of marketing; acquisitive efficiency in marketing; and social effectiveness in marketing. Since this book was written vast changes have been made in the way marketing is studied, both as regards the techniques of research used and the relative emphasis placed upon different parts of the subject. Much of what is done, however, is still based upon concepts and approaches assembled and, in considerable part, originated by this book.

In his third major work (published privately in 1949 as *Channel and Channel Group Costing*) Breyer concentrated his analysis on the marketing channel. The study was intended to be the first of a series to be issued under the general title *Quantita-Systemic Analysis and Control*; but he was unable to complete other studies in the series before his retirement.

His interest in the channel was first shown in *Commodity Marketing*, where channels are diagrammed for most of the commodities he considers. For some reason he hardly mentioned the term in *The Marketing Institution*, even though the concept is implicit in some of the charts there presented. He returned to channels because of a course he taught for some years concerned with distribution cost accounting, a study of vertical trade associations, and a comparison of bulk and package handling costs done for the American Management Association. He also saw in the analysis of channels an opportunity to build badly needed quantitative (as distinct from qualitative) studies of the marketing institution and its work. It all added up in his mind to the conviction expressed in his introduction to the 1949 report:

> A new fundamental approach to the whole study of marketing, that somehow hinged upon the marketing channel, could be developed that would make distinct contributions to our knowledge and mastery of this field over and above all present practical and theoretical approaches . . .

Channel and Channel Group Costing is not an easy book to read. Anyone working his way through it must be prepared to follow an author whose remorseless logic forces him to distinctions that are at once subtle and sharp as he seeks out entities subject to control by managers or regulators that are larger than the individual enterprise but smaller than the entire economy. Breyer himself would be the first to admit that he has succeeded in writing only a small fragment of the comprehensive report he visualized when he first set out on his quest. He is modest in his claims as to how many areas of business can be controlled by the methods he proposes. He has no illusions as to the difficulties facing anyone who undertakes to apply quantitative analysis to marketing by the use of his concepts.

His basic contribution to the study of marketing has nonetheless been a major one. An ever-increasing number of students seem to be accepting his basic idea that the study of channels and their control offers one of the most promising ways of understanding and controlling what goes on in marketing. Their opportunity to use the channel approach effectively is being enhanced by a concentration of the power to manage marketing into the hands of a rapidly diminishing number of decision centers. It is being enhanced even further by the opportunities computerization offers for assembling and analyzing vast masses of data derived from widely scattered sources. It can hardly be doubted that the years ahead will greatly expand opportunities for fruitful use of *channel analysis* both in theory and in practice. If this happens, it will be to Breyer that students must turn for many of the basic concepts and formulations with which they must work.

Norris Arthur Brisco
1876-1944

3

Norris Arthur Brisco
1876-1944

by JOHN W. WINGATE

AN ENTHUSIASTIC and forceful pioneer in the field of education for retailing, Norris A. Brisco made three major contributions to the retailing segment of marketing. First, he did a superlative job in "selling" retailing as a career to many college trained people. Second, he developed teachers for the new and growing field of retail education by providing fellowships and instructorships to students and graduates who showed particular promise. Third, he was instrumental in developing an entire library of college and high school texts for the new field of education.

A Canadian from Ontario, Brisco graduated from Queens University in 1898 with an A.B. and obtained his M.A. from the same institution in 1900. Columbia awarded him the Ph.D. degree in 1907. While working for this degree, he tutored at City College and became an Instructor of Economics there in 1907. The State University of Iowa called him as Professor of Commerce in 1915, and he became the Director of Iowa's School of Commerce in 1917.

A group of leading New York department store merchants, led by Percy Straus of Macy and Samuel Reyburn of Lord and Taylor, had in 1919 established at New York University a "Training School for Teachers of Retail Selling," and they were looking for a permanent head. It became quickly apparent that the School's destiny was to train operating and merchandising executives for retailing as well as teachers for schools and training departments. Norris A. Brisco was called in 1920 to become director of the new school and Professor of Merchandising; and the name of the school was changed to the School of Retailing, in order to give recognition to its broadened purpose.

Journal of Marketing
Vol. XXV No. 1, July, 1960
Reprinted by Permission

His close contact with the New York merchants developed in Brisco a tremendous enthusiasm for retailing as a career for college trained people. He succeeded in firing with his enthusiasm those who approached him for information about the new career field and those who heard him at his numerous speaking engagements. He had a retentive memory for the name and personal history of virtually everyone with whom he conversed and was ever ready with vocational guidance, tailor-made to the situation of the individual.

Norris A. Brisco had all the attributes of the top-notch salesman: his product was retailing—a field of many and varied opportunities. At a time when retailing was thought of as unworthy for the educated man, Brisco was a potent force in turning the tide of public opinion. The improved prestige that retailing enjoyed in the '40s may be attributed in part to his zeal. And it may be that the more recent decline in popularity may be attributed, in some measure, to a lack among present leaders of the enthusiasm Dean Brisco always imparted.

Along with his promotional activities, Brisco recognized the need to develop qualified teachers of retailing both for his own school and for the growing number of colleges and high schools that were fast introducing a retailing curriculum. He selected the most likely of his graduates, giving them great latitude to develop their own courses, their own training materials, and their own techniques. He insisted that they obtain their doctorates, at a time when this degree was not thought essential for business teaching, as it generally is today. Brisco's young teachers were made to feel that they were important pioneers in a great new movement. As a result, a large number of today's successful teachers of retailing are products of the New York University School of Retailing.

To many, Dean Brisco's major contribution to retailing was and is the founding and development of the Retailing Series, a whole library of texts on retail practice, published by Prentice-Hall, Inc. In 1920 there existed only two or three books that could be used as texts and they were not written for that purpose. In fact, there was very little text material in the whole field of business.

As early as 1913, Brisco himself had written what may be the first text in the field of business—*Economics of Business*—and he was now anxious to provide a more specialized literature. He recognized that he must develop a literature if retailing was to be taught and was to achieve the standards of a profession. Accordingly, he insisted that each member of his teaching staff be "productive"; to him this meant writing an acceptable text for some segment of the field. In many instances Brisco assumed the responsibility for organizing and rewriting the material and appeared as joint author with the person or persons he was developing. Between 1925 and 1942 he appeared as joint author of some nine collegiate and high school texts and as sole author of two others. Earlier in 1920 he had published two books of his own on Retail Salesmanship, before the Retailing Series was started. Probably his best known work is *Retailing*, published in 1935.

Brisco was also the driving force that led to the writing of some twelve additional books where he did not appear as joint author. These include John W. Wingate's *Manual of Retail Terms* and *Retail Merchandise Control*; John W. Wingate, Schaller, and Goldenthal's *Problems in Retail Merchandising* and *Workbook for Retail Buying and Marketing*; Robinson's *Retail Personnel Relations* and *Successful Retail Salesmanship*; Edwards and Howard's *Retail Advertising and Sales Promotion*; Isabel Wingate's *Textile Fabrics*; Isabel Wingate, Gillespie, and Addison's *Know Your Merchandise*; Bernice Chambers' *Color and Design*; Burris-Meyer's *Color and Design in the Decorative Arts*; Gladys Miller's *Decoratively Speaking* and Samuel Reyburn's *Selling Home Furnishings Successfully*.

Thus, about twenty-five important texts, many still appearing in revised editions can be attributed to the prodding drive of Norris A. Brisco.

Probably no other in the whole field of retail education did as much to "sell" retailing as a career, to develop teachers for the new field of education, and to provide a literature for the field.

Ralph Starr Butler
1882-1971

4

Ralph Starr Butler
1882-1971

by J.H. WESTING

No list of marketing pioneers would be complete that did not include the name of Ralph Starr Butler. He may not have blazed any trails in the sense of being the first to cover the ground, but he lengthened, straightened, and deepened several pioneering trails. Mr. Butler's unique genius lay not so much in creating but in organizing and systematizing what others had started. For example, he did not teach the first course in marketing, but he did author the first comprehensive book on the subject. He also appears to have been the first to have viewed the subject with the breadth and managerial emphasis that it is given today. Incidentally, Mr. Butler titled his first course and book *Marketing Methods,* a title perpetuated until very recent years on the course that he initiated at the University of Wisconsin. This modest title quite possibly would still be more accurate than the more ambitious *Principles of Marketing* so common today. Mr. Butler did not discover or even create much advertising, but he was one of the first to synthesize advertising practices into modern corporate practice in his work for the General Foods Corporation. Mr. Butler did not invent marketing research, but he did much to bring marketing research to bear on the planning and execution of advertising programs. In fact, his contributions to advertising were so far-reaching that the New York World-Telegram once denominated him "the No. 1 ad man."

Ralph Starr Butler graduated from the University of Michigan in 1904. After graduation he taught commercial subjects in high school for a year and a half in Racine, Wisconsin. Following this teaching stint he went to New York to run that office of the Chicago Teachers' Agency. This job soon palled on him and after a few months Mr. Butler entered business with the Herring-Hall-

This sketch was written especially for this collection in lieu of the one appearing in Vol. XXV No. 4, April 7, 1961, issue of the Journal of Marketing.

Marvin Safe Company in New York. In 1907 he transferred to the Procter and Gamble Company where he first practiced marketing as the assistant to the eastern sales manager in Cincinnati. Mr. Butler stayed with Procter and Gamble for about three years and in 1910 accepted an appointment as Assistant Professor at the University of Wisconsin.

During the six years Ralph Starr Butler spent at the University of Wisconsin he made most of the academic contributions which he contributed to the field. His first assignment was to develop a number of correspondence study courses in the various functional areas. When he got to the area of marketing he found that there was little literature extant. Consequently he began to develop a series of pamphlets on marketing subjects which formed the basis for a course entitled Marketing Methods. In 1911 these pamphlets were revised and published by the Alexander Hamilton Institute as part of the fourth volume of their first series of textbooks under the title *Selling and Buying*. This material became the basis for a resident course entitled Marketing Methods. In a couple of years the material was revised and extended into a textbook with the same title. Professor H.H. Maynard of Ohio State University said of this book that it "must be considered one of the most influential of the early contributions to this field." Mr. Butler himself said by way of interpreting his intentions that "I developed the idea that personal salesmanship and advertising had to do simply with the final expression of the selling idea. My experience with the Procter and Gamble Company had convinced me that a manufacturer seeking to market a product had to consider and solve a large number of problems before he ever gave expression to the selling idea. . . . In brief, the subject matter that I intended to treat was to include a study of everything that the promoter of a product has to do prior to his actual use of salesmen and advertising."

After six years, and promotion to Associate Professor, Mr. Butler left the University of Wisconsin to return to New York. For a year he was a member of the New York University staff and then, in 1917, he transferred to business as Director of Commerical Research for the United States Rubber Company. He stayed with the company until 1926 holding various positions, including that of Advertising Manager. In 1926, he joined the Post Company as Advertising Manager where he was responsible for many of the promotional ideas that made their cereals and Postum highly successful brands. In 1929, the General Foods merger was completed and Ralph Starr Butler became Vice President in Charge of Advertising of the new and much larger company. In this capacity he helped launch a host of new products, pioneered several types of radio entertainment, sponsored some of the advertising agencies which eventually became nationally known, and pioneered the comic strip form of advertising. Eventually, in 1938, Mr. Butler assumed corporate responsibility for public relations, research and development, and the General Foods kitchens.

His peers in advertising recognized and acknowledged his eminence in their field. In 1940, he was awarded the Silver Medal Annual Advertising Award and in 1947, he was awarded the Gold Medal. In 1948, the Advertising Club of New York gave Ralph Starr Butler its Bronze Plaque. The American Marketing Associating gave him its award of distinction in 1949 in recognition of his original work in teaching and the practice of marketing. Colorado College, which he attended as an undergraduate, awarded him an honorary doctor's degree in 1954.

Over the years the writer had three personal experiences with Ralph Starr Butler and each of the three is clearly etched in his memory. The first occasion was when, as a young case writer, I was sent to New York to get the marketing story behind the consolidation of the several independent companies into the General Foods Corporation. I found Mr. Butler in a magnificent office on one of the upper floors of the Post building on Park Avenue. He was flanked by secretaries in rooms on both sides, and to this fledgling case writer, seemed impregnable and unapproachable. After reconnoitering the stronghold for several minutes I finally approached one of the secretaries and was duly ushered into the presence of Mr. Butler who immediately put me at my ease. Soon he picked up his telephone and told his secretaries that he was not to be disturbed. Mr. Butler spent the entire day with me and not only gave me one of the best cases of my short case-writing career, but earned my permanent respect as a scholarly gentleman.

The second occasion was when he was visiting his alma mater and I had the pleasure of interviewing him on a radio program. As we were walking to the studio he asked me who was to be the next president of the University. I told him that it would almost certainly be Mr. X, the Vice-President, because he had been brought to the University with this in prospect. Mr. Butler asked me how long he had been in his position and when I said about six years he commented, "Don't bet on it. It's dangerous to be crown prince too long." Mr. X did not become President and I have often recalled Mr. Butler's comment when other obvious heir-apparents have been passed over.

The third experience was one day when Mr. Butler came to Madison and I had him talk to a marketing class. The subject got around to private brands and this was back when they were a newer phenomenon and the dominance and price of Jell-o was being challenged by A & P's Sparkle. In reply to a question concerning the threat that private brands posed to national brands Mr. Butler leaned back, thought for a moment, and said: "Private brands are so important to consumers and the economy that if they did not exist I'd invent them." It seemed to me this was a statesmanlike statement for a man whose life was being bedeviled by the very thing he was commending.

Ralph Starr Butler officially retired from the General Foods Corporation in 1948 but he stayed on in a quasi-official capacity for several years as company historian and senior statesman. He died at his home in Bronxville, N.Y. on March 19, 1971. The field of marketing, and the practice of advertising are much the richer for his having lived.

Paul Terry Cherington
1876-1943

5

Paul Terry Cherington
1876-1943

by ARCHIBALD M. CROSSLEY

On the evening of April 25, 1939, nearly 160 friends of Paul Cherington met at the Hotel Ambassador in New York to honor him with a testimonial dinner. The occasion was commemorative of 30 years of leadership in scientific marketing dating back to the start of his Harvard Business School courses in "Commercial Organization and Method" and in "Economic Resources of the United States," which later became "Marketing." He taught at the Business School for over ten years.

Dean Gay in the early years of the School discovered Mr. Cherington as an employee of the Philadelphia Commercial Museum in 1908, with a Master's degree from the University of Pennsylvania, a large fund of interesting information on commercial subjects, and a notably retentive memory. His earliest job was akin to industry, as Assistant Editor from 1897-1902 of *The Manufacturer,* published by the Manufacturers Club of Philadelphia, which he left to become editor of the publications of the Commercial Museum. He was born in Ottawa, Kansas, on October 31, 1876; attended Ohio Wesleyan University 1893-1897; and received a B.S. from the University of Pennsylvania in 1902 and an A.M. in 1908. He married Marie Louise Richards of Montclair, New Jersey, in 1911 and his two sons, Charles and Paul, are now both Harvard professors.

Paul Cherington's career as a nationally known authority on marketing and distribution gained impetus when in 1918 he began work with the textile section of the division of planning and statistics of the U.S. Shipping Board, Washington. His specialization in textiles continued as he became Secretary-Treasurer of the National

Journal of Marketing
Vol. XXI No. 2, October, 1956
Reprinted by Permission

Association of Wool Manufacturers, Boston, and editor of their Quarterly Bulletin, 1919-1922. In 1922 he began his long and outstanding period of service as Director of Research for the J. Walter Thompson Company advertising agency, where he edited five editions of *Population and Its Distribution,* which was given the Bok Award in 1931. For a year he taught marketing and distribution at the Stanford University Graduate School of Business, and for three years he lectured on marketing at New York University.

The milestones marked by his presence were numerous. One of the pioneer books on advertising was his "Advertising as a Business Force" in 1913. His early analysis of the importance of the functions in marketing appeared in his "Elements of Marketing" published in 1920. As early as 1914 he was Chairman of a Committee of the United States Chamber of Commerce on maintenance of resale prices. Later, as Chairman of the Chamber's Subcommittee on the Census of Distribution and member of the Committee on Wholesale Distribution, Cherington played a major role in the establishment of the distribution censuses. He served some years as a member of the Advisory Committee on Metropolitan Districts 1938-1940. He was recognized as among the first to establish qualitative methods of opinion testing. *The Fortune Survey,* one of the leading public opinion polls, grew out of his association in business with Roper and Wood. In 1939 he became a partner in the firm of McKinsey and Company, serving as a consultant to leading corporations on problems of marketing, pricing policies, and distribution. He was with this company when he died in 1943.

Paul Cherington was elected the first president of the American Marketing Association at its formation in 1931 and was also president of the National Association of Teachers of Marketing and Advertising, the Market Research Council, and the New York Chapter of the Society for the Advancement of Management. A man of quiet, unassuming nature, Paul had a never-failing sense of humor, which one of his many friends once described as a "faint twinkle and an infectious Cherington chuckle behind an intellectual expression." Studious and meticulous, he had his own carefully catalogued library of well over a thousand business volumes. He was chosen for the Boston Distribution Conference "Hall of Fame," and in 1949 the Paul D. Converse National Award was bestowed upon him posthumously as one of the "pioneer scholars who established the foundations for scientific work in marketing."

Leading a memorial tribute at the American Marketing Association, his old associate, Elmo Roper, said: "The monument he has left is inside the people who knew him. He has passed on to you and to me, to his students at Harvard, to his clients, and all of the many associates he has had a certain measure of additional vision, a certain measure of additional insight and tolerance, and a certain measure of additional courage to go on and make the field in which he worked so long and so hard and so well a profession in the highest and best sense of the word."

Fred Emerson Clark
1890-1948

6

Fred Emerson Clark
1890-1948

by R.M. CLEWETT

FRED EMERSON CLARK, the American Marketing Association's second president and its first from the academic field, earned his position of eminence in marketing through his scholarly writings and his wide influence as a teacher. His ability to make friends of all he met greatly increased the sphere of his influence.

Clark grew up in Albion, Michigan, graduated from Albion College, and went to the University of Illinois for graduate work in Economics where he attained the Ph.D. degree in 1916. After teaching appointments at Delaware College and the University of Michigan, Clark became a member of the faculty at Northwestern University where he remained until his death.

His major publication, *Principles of Marketing*, first published in 1922, focused attention on Clark. In this volume he developed a framework of reference that remained useful to his students and colleagues for many years. Moreover, he succeeded in bringing to his readers and students a greater appreciation of the potentialities of and need for more analysis in a field characterized for the most part by description. His pioneering text remained a leader in its field for over twenty years in this country and abroad. It was translated into Japanese and published as a two-volume work in 1929. In 1924 he brought out *Readings in Marketing* as a means of bringing to students a select group of current descriptive articles to supplement his basic text.

Clark's second major publication, in collaboration with L.D.H. Weld, was *Marketing Agricultural Products in the United States*, (1932). This volume served for several years as a leading text and reference volume in agricultural marketing.

Journal of Marketing
Vol. XXII No. l, July, l957
Reprinted by Permission

As a recognized authority in marketing he prepared, as author or co-author, articles for the *Encyclopaedia Britannica.*

Less conspicuous but equally important were Clark's contributions as a speaker and a teacher. For over thirty years he helped to mold potential marketing teachers and executives, many of whom are prominent today. Students will remember him as a wise and skillful discussion leader who stimulated and encouraged independent thinking; a lecturer whose well-organized presentations of theory were influenced by the practical wisdom of one in touch with the realities of business and government; an understanding teacher and friend whose interest in students continued long after their university training was ended.

He made a determined effort to develop younger men by providing them guidance and opportunity to work on their own. His graduate students will remember the time and effort he devoted to bringing them in close touch with the leaders in the field at professional meetings. The contacts he was able to share with his students arose in part through his active role in the American Marketing Association and its predecessor, the National Association of Teachers of Marketing and Advertising.

In addition to his work as a consultant in marketing and sales administration to nationally known firms and as an expert witness in the court proceedings resulting in the Packers' Consent decree, Clark also served as a code authority and in other capacities under the National Recovery Administration.

From 1944 to 1946 he served as an advisor and committee chairman for the Committee on Economic Development. At the time of his death, he was Staff Economist of the Subcommittee on Trade Policies of the United States Senate Committee on Interstate and Foreign Commerce then engaged in investigating basing-point pricing

Clark was fortunate in having the able assistance of his wife. Having been trained as a librarian and having earned a Master's degree, Mrs. Clark was a great assistance in the preparation of the 1942 revision of *Principles of Marketing.* In recognition of this, her name was carried as co-author.

Recognition in the form of professional awards came to Clark posthumously. In 1949 he was the recipient of the American Marketing Association's coveted Paul D. Converse Award for outstanding contributions to science in marketing and in 1953 was elected to the Distribution Hall of Fame of the Boston Conference on Distribution.

Fred Clark was a man of high ethical standards, a careful scholar, an outstanding teacher, and a developer of men. His influence in the field of marketing is still being felt through the men he developed, the conceptual framework he provided.

Paul Dulaney Converse
1889-1968

7

Paul Dulaney Converse
1889-1968

by HARVEY W. HUEGY

The retirement of Professor Paul D. Converse in September, 1957, occurred after thirty-three years on the University of Illinois faculty, and a total of forty-five years of active teaching. His professional career constitutes a bridge from the nascent beginnings of a new area of academic inquiry to the present highly organized and respected study of a well established field of academic interest.

Paul Converse studied at Washington and Lee University where he received his Baccalaureate degree in 1913, and his Master of Arts and Certificate in Commerce in 1914; in 1944 his alma mater honored him with an LL.D. He also studied at Columbia and Wisconsin during the summers of 1914, 1915, and 1916. His teaching career began in 1912 when, at the age of 23, he taught at Washington and Lee. In 1915 he moved to the University of Pittsburgh and left there in 1924 to join the faculty of the University of Illinois. While always a teacher he made brief excursions into government service, working with the Federal Trade Commission from 1917 to 1919 and again in 1934, and with the Department of Commerce in 1945.

During his early teaching he covered such diverse subjects as economics, transportation accounting, statistics, foreign trade, commercial geography, public debating, management, and marketing. This early experience provided him with an unusual breadth of view. During these early years he established the habit of seeking information by personal observation and by asking questions of businessmen. This was almost a necessity for the early teachers of business subjects, especially marketing, since there was little available in the form of published materials. That we are now more plentifully supplied is, in very large part, the result of the work and efforts of Converse and his contemporaries.

As a graduate student at Wisconsin he had a course with Ralph Starr Butler. This was his only formal training in marketing before he started teaching the subject. Even that course was called management, although it did include some lectures on marketing. At Wisconsin he knew Richard T. Ely, William Scott, and Benjamin Hibbard and they also stimulated his thinking about marketing and economics. He was also a member of the group who formed one of the professional marketing associations which preceded and was later merged into the American Marketing Association. He was always an active member of the association and served as president in 1931. The American Marketing Association honored him further by establishing in his name an award for contributions to marketing thought.

As a scholar and writer Converse's career is amazingly and continuously productive. In 1921 he published his first general marketing text. *Marketing Methods and Policies,* and revised it in 1924. *Selling Policies* appeared in 1927. The first edition of *Elements of Marketing,* which has had six editions to date, was published in 1930. In 1936 he wrote *Essentials of Distribution,* and in 1948, *Introduction to Marketing.*

Production of these major books would, in itself, constitute a complete and very active professional career. For "P.D." this was but a fraction of his activity and of his interest. He engaged in a series of research inquiries examining trade movements. His research on Reilly's Law contributed greatly to this important tool of marketing. He pioneered in the investigation of consumer behavior and purchase patterns and influences. He gave attention to the cost of marketing, commodity marketing, and marketing institutions such as auctions, chains, and wholesalers. He contributed to a wide variety of journals on an even wider variety of topics. The bibliographical record of his writings includes six books, ten monographic research studies, and fifty-eight articles, in addition to numerous book reviews and articles in trade papers and other sources.

"P.D." had been generous in extending to younger colleagues an invitation to collaborate. Joint authorship has been shown in many instances when a footnote of acknowledgement would have been more accurate. Many young graduate students have been encouraged to make their initial venture into print through his suggestions, criticism, and active aid.

In his teaching "P.D." brought to the classroom the results of his own original research, supplementing the texts from his rich fund of personal experiences drawn from a seemingly inexhaustible memory. His familiarity with the literature was an inspiration, and his strong feeling for practicality enabled him to develop both the practice and theory of marketing. He has a respect for and command of detail; he combines this with the ability to generalize soundly. His classes were informal, for he enlivened the lectures with anecdote and reminiscence. He was always an exacting teacher; a diligent worker himself, he demanded hard work from his students.

His influence on students will continue beyond the life of the printed books. Many are now teachers of marketing because his interest, enthusiasm, and breadth of scholarship stimulated them to know more about the subject of marketing. Many are better teachers because "P.D." guided them when they were first introduced to the subject. He steered them wisely and well, and they will extend his influence to future generations of students.

One of Converse's outstanding characteristics is intellectual curiosity. He has an inquiring mind and is ingenious in finding ways to get answers. The early experience of finding out about marketing by inquiry of those who were engaged in marketing has remained strong. Literally thousands of businessmen have contributed marketing information in response to his penetrating questions. Even on vacation he interviews people about marketing, observes an unusual marketing method, or inquires about a new problem. Research and inquiry are not sedentary activities for him—he is always asking why and always seeking to find out for himself. Throughout his career he accomplished a large amount of research and with practically no research funds.

He is an objective thinker, but even more rare he is objective about himself and his own work. In part this stems from sincere humility, in part from a sense of humor. He was always himself—never pretending to be something he was not and hesitant to claim to be all that he was.

Although he worked intensively and long hours, his love of people permitted him to relax easily. He could lay aside the work to visit and to show his interest in the problems of others. Students found him accessible and ready to consult with them. Colleagues have found him helpful with his time. He knows how to play as well as work, and thus has found the rewards of a balanced life full of human experiences.

Converse's stature and reputation, together with others of his generation, make it appear that there were giants in those days. With the accumulation of knowledge it is difficult for any member of the current generation to loom so large or to command a field of knowledge so completely. Today there are numerous scholars of ability, but they are numerous because of the contribution to their development made by the founders of scientific marketing.

Editors' Afternote: Professor Huegy provided the following paragraph for inclusion in this volume:

For Professor Converse retirement did not mean inactivity; he accepted a number of invitations to visiting professorships at universities from Texas to Oregon. While at Texas in 1959 he authored monographs on Marketing Thought and Marketing History. He never lost his intellectual curiosity and interest, especially in marketing theory, and at the time of his death he was working on a manuscript in the area of theory. Unfortunately this work was not completed at the time of his death, October 13, 1968.

Melvin T. Copeland
1884-

8

Melvin T. Copeland
1884-

by MALCOLM P. McNAIR

Probably as much as any single individual, Melvin T. Copeland gave shape and direction to Marketing as it is taught in schools and colleges throughout the United States today. In the development at Harvard, others were associated during the early days of the Business School—particularly Dean Edwin F. Gay, Mr. Arch W. Shaw, and Professor Paul T. Cherington—but it was Copeland who evolved the characteristic structure of the Harvard Marketing course, with its emphasis on the consumer as the central focus, its pre-eminent concern with dynamic rather than static aspects, and its organization along the lines of business management functions rather than physical tasks or economic functions.

In this last connection, it may be remarked that Copeland, though trained as an economist, struck boldly away from economic theory as a basis for Marketing. Throughout his career he has always held to the view that marketing has more to contribute to economic theory than economic theory has to contribute to marketing. It is consistent with this thinking that Copeland in 1924 in his *Principles of Merchandising* tried to lay some foundation stones for marketing theory in his formulation of consumer buying habits and consumer buying motives. He has long since recognized that some of these early generalizations were premature, but it cannot be denied that they pointed toward the type of exploration of marketing theory that is in full swing today.

Intimately connected with the evolution of the marketing course during the formative period of the Harvard Business School were two other activities in which Copeland was likewise the central figure, namely, the studies of retail and wholesale operating costs

Journal of Marketing
Vol. XXII No. 2, October, 1957
Reprinted by Permission

and the development of the case method of instruction.

The pioneer endeavor of its kind anywhere in the world was the undertaking of the newly established Bureau of Business Research in 1911 to find out the costs of running shoe stores. Copeland himself has commented as follows on the significance of this initial project:

> The whole field of distribution costs was virgin territory for study. A start could have been made almost anywhere, but instead of spending time in a canvass of where to begin, the retail shoe trade was picked, more or less arbitrarily, for the opening wedge.
>
> That administrative decision had broad significance not only for the development of research at the Harvard Business School but also for business research in general and for other types of research as well. Instead of starting out to study the whole field of distribution costs at one time or even to try to cover the entire retail field, the undertaking was narrowed down to *one* trade. It did not matter greatly which trade was selected. The important thing was to limit the study to a sufficiently narrow area to have a chance of obtaining some significant data within a reasonable period of time. That was the first application of a principle which has continued for over forty years to be followed in the School's research activities—namely, what later came to be called the "pedestrian" or "step-by-step" approach. It is a slow process and requires great patience, but the results of using that approach are likely to be more lasting than those of an omnibus type of research.[1]

Copeland was not the first Director of the Bureau of Business Research. (That was Dr. Selden O. Martin.) But when the Bureau's second venture—a study of retail grocery store costs—was launched in 1914, Copeland was given responsibility for this project; and in 1916 he became Director of the Bureau. With the resumption of research following the close of World War I, Copeland vigorously led the Bureau during its period of greatest activity, up to the middle 1920's. The importance of such collection of distribution cost data as a means of providing a factual foundation for the study of marketing, as well as other business subjects, was rapidly perceived; and Bureaus of Business Research soon became part of the organization of many schools of business.

Even as early as 1920, however, Copeland's own interest had begun to more toward what he regarded as an even more important experiment than the distribution cost studies. That experiment was the case method of instruction, a development that had been incubating at Harvard ever since the opening of the Business School in 1908. Copeland has sketched the sequence of events that led to the publication of the first case book, his *Problems in Marketing,* in 1920:

> In 1912 Dean Gay made the move whereby one section of the course in Commercial Organization (later renamed Marketing) came to be conducted on a discussion basis. The situations discussed were ones presented, for the most part, in rather general terms in the books and articles assigned to the students to read, or derived from such assignments. Those situations were not cases, in the later sense, but there was continuous discussion. Progress was made, nevertheless, even though it was slow. From the crude start in 1912 an outline of the subject was developed and material gradually was assembled which made possible the publication of the first business case book in 1920.
>
> The editor of the first Marketing case book was favored by certain circumstances. In the first place, over the preceeding seven years he had hammered out what seemed to him to be a systematic outline of his subject. Hence his task was to find or conceive realistic situations which had come to his attention through the contacts of the Bureau of Business Research, through other contacts with businessmen, and through articles and reports published in various business magazines, government reports, and so on. In the third place, the editor had had the experience of conducting classes in Marketing, Business Statistics, and European Trade by the discussion method for five years from 1912 to 1917 and in the special session in 1919. He had learned some points on what is conducive to a lively and profitable discussion in the classroom.

Although by present standards many of the cases in the 1920 *Problems in Marketing* book were sketchy and fragmentary, this case book proved from the start to be an effective teaching instrument; and three subsequent editions following rapidly in the next ten years exhibited marked improvement in the quality and range of the case material.

Strictly in the area of marketing, Copeland's contribution culminated in this period. As his own words intimate, it was essentially a contribution growing out of a union of the three activities in the formative period of the Harvard Business School which all revolved around him as the central actor, namely, the creation of the Marketing course, the studies of retail and wholesale operating costs, and the development of the case method of instruction.

At least equal in importance with his contribution to education generally is his profound influence on the case method. Following the publication of *Problems in Marketing* in 1920, Dean Donham moved vigorously to effect the conversion of the entire curriculum to the case method, and as the most practical means of obtaining case material quickly he centralized the collection of cases in the Bureau of Business Research under Copeland's direction. Thus, in this formative period of case development, Copeland's ideas were profoundly influential in shaping the techniques both of writing and of using cases. Although case collection was decentralized in 1926, the Copeland tradition of case writing and case teaching continued to be powerful for a long time. In recent years there have been many new developments of importance in the writing and use of cases, but it still remains true that the basic foundation was laid in the period when Copeland's influence was dominant.

Aside from the marketing books already alluded to, Copeland's publications have ranged over several other fields: cotton textile manufacturing and merchandising, statistics, raw commodity prices, and the functions of directors and business executives. Also, in this busy multiplicity of academic work, he found time for useful public service, notably as Executive Secretary of the Conservation Division of the War Industries Board in World War I and as Chairman of the Massachusetts Committee on Post-War Readjustment during World War II. Other activities, which have continued into retirement, include business consulting on marketing and administrative problems and a Trusteeship of Bowdoin College.

At 72, "Doc" Copeland is still vigorous, both mentally and physically, and his contributions are by no means ended. But whatever the future holds, his greatest contribution will be the men that he has developed. Such educators as President Malott of Cornell, President Baker of Ohio University, Dean Richard Donham at Northwestern, Dean Culliton at Notre Dame, and Dean David, recently retired from Harvard, all in one sense or another have been Doc Copeland's "boys," as have such members of the Harvard Business School Faculty as Neil Borden, Edmund Learned, George Albert Smith, and the late Charles Gragg. Through these and others whom he trained and inspired, as well as by his own particular accomplishments, Melvin T. Copeland has made a lasting imprint on both business school and college education in the United States.

Editors' Afternote: Professor McNair provided the following paragraph for inclusion in this volume:

Fifteen years after the preparation of the foregoing biographical note and eighteen years after Copeland's retirement from the Harvard Business School, it is a pleasure to report that he is still vigorous in mind and body, living by himself in Annisquam, Mass., in a house directly on the ocean, taking long walks, and active in nature study and local historical investigation. His most recent public appearance was at the 50th Reunion of the Harvard Business School Class of 1922, the two years in which the major swing to the case method was initiated.

---

[1] *And Mark an Ear: The Story of the Harvard Business School,* Little Brown, 1958.

Henry E. Erdman
1884-

9

Henry E. Erdman
1884-

by GEORGE L. MEHREN

For more than four decades Henry E. Erdman has been a leader in Agricultural Economics. He is one of the pioneers in research and teaching in the area of agricultural and food marketing. Through his research, his teaching, and his counsel to agricultural marketing organizations, Dr. Erdman has influenced the development of agricultural co-operatives as much as any other man in the nation.

Over the years Professor Erdman has assembled at the University of California an excellent collection of historical material with respect to co-operatives in California. He has built both his teaching and his research in all areas of marketing upon a process of direct observation, visiting and revisiting markets throughout the country, notebook in pocket. He has always kept close contact with people in the trade and in government as well as with colleagues in the universities.

Dr. Erdman was born and reared on a grain and livestock farm in South Dakota. He took a B.S. degree from South Dakota State College, majoring in dairy industry. Here the pattern of direct participation and observation which has persisted throughout a long and fruitful career was set. He was a butter maker, and served as State Dairy Inspector prior to undertaking graduate work at the University of Wisconsin where he finished his Ph.D. in 1920.

In 1917 Professor Erdman was an Assistant Professor of Rural Economics, teaching and doing research in marketing at the College of Agriculture in the Ohio State College. In 1921 he became Chief of the Cost of Marketing Division in the Bureau of Markets in the U.S. Department of Agriculture at Washington. Thus, he has been a pioneer in the teaching and governmental phases of agricultural marketing.

Journal of Marketing
Vol. XXIV No. 4, April, 1960
Reprinted by Permission

In 1922, when Elwood Mead was building a Department of Rural Institutions at the University of California at Berkeley, Henry Erdman was appointed Associate Professor of Rural Institutions. Thirty years later he retired as Professor of Agricultural Economics, and Agricultural Economist in the Experiment Station and on the Giannini Foundation. Dr. Erdman directed the first economic outlook studies for California crop and livestock products, believing that such work might help producers to adjust their production to market demands. From this idea, there blossomed a series of quantitative studies by Professors Voorhies, Wellman, Rauchenstein, Gould, and others which may have set a tone for the positivist and quantitative emphasis that has long marked the work of the Giannini Foundation.

Dr. Erdman also was active in the area of national agricultural policy as early as 1925. With outlook studies designed to indicate to farmers prospective adjustments before being forced to make them, Professor Erdman long emphasized that policy should be based on recognition that production or marketing improvements tend to be diffused throughout the entire economy and that farmers can, in fact, make major and minor adjustments in their operations. He always has held that policy makers should encourage individual adjustments—he calls it "assisted laissez-faire."

Dr. Erdman helped to found the San Francisco Chapter of the American Marketing Association and was its third President. He was President of the Western Farm Economics Association, and 18th President of the American Farm Economic Association. He edited the *Journal of Farm Economics* for two years. He was Program Director for the International Conference on Agricultural and Co-operative Credit. He has long been an active and outstanding member of the Commonwealth Club of San Francisco. In addition to his formal research, he has given countless addresses to all kinds of audiences with respect to co-operative marketing. In conjunction with the late E.A. Stokdyk, he developed a widely used correspondence course in co-operative marketing.

Since 1917 Dr. Erdman has written two books, more than 125 articles for professional journals and a variety of other outlets, 10 major research bulletins, and about 15 other publications that have appeared as circulars, chapters in books, and various types of technical reports. More than 65 of his publications have dealt with agricultural co-operation. His writings cover types of co-operative organization, experience with price control and marketing orders, operating problems, relationships of research and marketing agencies, advertising and promotion, demand analysis, and, perhaps most important, co-operative finance. He is especially recognized for his work in revolving finance plans. Taken together, his work provides probably the best basis for appraisal of the needs for co-operative activity; and means for evaluating the benefits of co-operative activity. He has had a continuous interest in the history of co-operative marketing organization, and at present is at work on a book which should provide the definitive history of agricultural co-operatives in California.

His two books have been major contributions to the literature of marketing. In 1921 he published *The Marketing of Whole Milk,* and in 1928 *American Produce Markets.* Both books are still widely used. The writing here — typical of all of Dr. Erdman's work — is concise and clear. The milk study has been an example to later research workers in developing the theoretical or logical structure of analysis. He is also one of the pioneers in the economics of produce exchange, transportation, and standardization in marketing.

Dr. Erdman's conclusions are cautiously stated until the research basis for definitive statement becomes compelling. He has always required of himself that he know the details of the marketing institutions and procedures with which he has dealt. He has never stood clear of controversial issues. His attitudes toward his work, his students, his friends, and perhaps toward life in general have always been critical, but also genial and utterly free of malice. With respect to co-operatives, he has pointed out that they can be of benefit in improving and standardizing grades and packs, in orienting production of marketing processes, in controlling flows to market, in developing one basic thesis—that benefits from improvements tend to disappear rather quickly and to be diffused throughout the economic system.

His recent writings clearly reflect an awareness of the structural changes occuring in food and agricultural marketing. His "Progress Calls for Readjustment," in the *Journal of Farm Economics* in 1954, and "Principles of Co-operation," which he wrote with J.M. Tinley in 1957, point out that a co-operative "must continuously adjust its operation to new conditions." Henry Erdman himself has always adjusted to the changing facts of economic life.

This is a man who began his teaching and his research in a difficult and complex field at a time when he virtually stood alone. For thirty years he has been a leader. His greatest contribution—possibly—is to a large number of students who have trained under him. Without exception, these students have carried respect and affection for Henry Erdman as man and scholar.

Editors' Afternote: Dr. Mehren provided the following paragraphs for inclusion in this volume:

Henry Erdman lives and works with zest and competence today, as he has lived and worked for all the years of a fruitful and happy life. He keeps his house in the Berkeley hills. It is a happy house because he is a happy man. He keeps his office and he works now as he always has worked. His scope of interest ranges from stock markets to produce markets to politics. His friends are young and old and of every persuasion.

Henry Erdman is a successful teacher and scientist and man not merely because he is a competent technician. He keeps the spark of creativity today that for so many years led him first to ask the questions that needed to be asked and then to find answers that could be put to use. Ray Bressler, who was himself a distinguished economist, once said that Henry Erdman always did it first, and better.

Few men have been so productive for so many years. Few men have lived a better life or given more to others.

Edward A. Filene 1860-1937
and
Lincoln Filene 1865-1957

10

Edward A. Filene 1860-1937 and Lincoln Filene 1865-1957

by DANIEL BLOOMFIELD

The contributions to the advancement of retail distribution made by Edward Albert Filene and Lincoln Filene through their world-famous store in Boston are a significant chapter in the history of marketing in this country. Their long-range vision encompassed some major pioneering ideas which set the stage for important progress in their field. Their unusually broad conception of the part their store should play in its sphere of activity and their sense of personal responsibility and duty to their organization and to the community made these men distinguished figures whose influence will long be felt.

"E.A," as Edward Filene was called, and Lincoln and their associates developed the Filene organization to the point where it became one of the greatest institutions for effective distribution and the largest specialty store in the world. Under their leadership the store made significant advances in methods of merchandising.

One such innovation was EA's idea of the *Automatic Bargain Basement*, first used in 1909, whose unique method of operation has never been successfully duplicated elsewhere. Merchandise, under this plan, has to be sold in 30 selling days. It is first marked at a bargain price. If it is not sold within 12 selling days, the price is automatically reduced 25 per cent, and another 25 per cent at the end of 18 selling days; then still another 25 per cent reduction is made after 24 selling days. If the merchandise remains unsold after 30 days, it is given to charity. The skill with which the buyers select goods for basement sale (odd lots, manufacturers' surplus, remainders from leading stores, stocks of bankrupts, etc.) is such that

Journal of Marketing
Vol. XXIII No. 3, January, 1959
Reprinted by Permission

very little remains at the end of the 30-day period.

The Model Stock Plan is another innovation in merchandising initiated by EA in 1925 and described in his book *The Model Stock Plan* (1930). The idea of this plan is "having the right goods, at the right prices, in the right quantities, at the right time."

The Filene brothers had a keen interest in scientific management. They believed that facts are the essential ingredient in judgment. EA, in his book *Next Steps Forward in Retailing* (1937), said that "thinking based on fact finding is more important than traditional experience." He constantly emphasized the importance of collecting facts and interpreting them. He stressed the need of applying scientific management to large scale operation, involving research as the first and fundamental principle.

EA believed that the future belongs to large-scale retailing. For most successful large-scale management, he said, we need a combination of two main types — the chain store and the department store. His philosophy is expressed in his statement that "mas production is not simply large-scale production. It is large scale production bases upon a clear understanding that increased production demands increased buying, and that the greatest total profits can be obtained only if the masses can and do enjoy a higher and ever higher standard of living." In his Foreword to E.A. Filene's book *Successful Living in This Machine Age* (1931), Glenn Frank said: "More than any other American, he foresaw and formulated the social significance of mass production and mass distribution, if and when these processes are subjected to statesmanlike direction."

EA believed that "the challenge to American retailers is given by mass distribution and calls for a change from shopkeeping to mass distribution, better service to the consumer, cutting high costs of distribution, because scientific large-scale management will help eliminate the sources of the enormous waste in present-day distribution and give the consumers the best values for their dollar." Mass distribution, he said, does not necessarily mean large corporations. "It means that consumer wants will be satisfied by the most efficient methods at lowest possible costs."

EA pointed out that small independent stores could be efficient outlets of mass distribution if organized as "voluntary chains," pooling their purchases and centralizing policies and functions such as merchandising, advertising and research. To be most successful they must apply scientific management.

He believed in the credit-union idea and gave substantial sums to the organization which is now nation-wide. His interest in economic advance led him to establish and endow The Twentieth Century Fund. He also established the Edward A. Filene Good Will Fund, Inc., to be used in encouraging organization of consumer co-operative department stores—a project that has had little growth to date.

EA firmly believed in the importance of people of various nations learning to know each other. He sparked the idea of "tourist-class" transportation on ocean liners, which became highly successful. He made trips to Europe an annual affair, meeting heads of government, important merchants and others interested in world affairs and progress. He conceived the idea, now used universally, of the device for simultaneous translation of speeches in various languages with individual earphones for listeners. The author accompanied EA to London in 1921 to the first meeting of the International Chamber of Commerce where this device was initiated.

EA was a powerful influence in the formation of the International Chamber of Commerce, also of the Chamber of the United States and The Boston Chamber of Commerce. It was his belief that businessmen should organize for their common good, for the promotion of standards of doing business and making the community a better place in which to live and do business.

Edward Filene was a dynamic personality whose ideas and vision of the future of retail distribution were a sharp challenge to those satisfied with the status quo. He and his brother, Lincoln, firmly believed that their store was an instrument for public service. EA was impatient of time in seeing his ideas carried out. He was a prolific reader of modern economic literature and that dealing with civic and foreign affairs. He believed that the essence of progress is constructive change.

Though different in temperament, EA and Lincoln Filene supplemented each other with an unusual combination of qualities which marked the success of the Filene enterprise and contributed substantially to the advance of retail distribution.

Lincoln made his contribution through his influence on the personnel in his organization. The selection and training of people for the jobs of merchandising was one of his major interests. This led to his strong support in launching the movement to establish personnel administration on a professional basis, and its widespread development. It all began in 1909 when The Vocational Bureau of Boston, headed by Meyer Bloomfield who worked closely with Mr. Filene, called together fifty men engaged in hiring people in shops and stores, to consider the advisability of meeting regularly and exchanging experience. They organized the Employment Managers Association. This was the impetus which led other cities to organize similar groups to give special attention to personnel administration as a vital factor, not only in the field of retail distribution but in business and industry generally. Ernest Martin Hopkins, who later became President of Dartmouth College, was engaged by Lincoln Filene to act as Employment Manager of the store.

The vocational-guidance movement also had its beginning with The Vocation Bureau to which Lincoln Filene gave substantial time and support. Filene then encouraged action in advancing vocational education with the aim of making production and distribution more efficient. This led to his sustained interest in business education as a means of training men for executive positions and leadership. For many years he served on the Visiting Committee of the Harvard Business School. His friends established the Lincoln Filene Chair in Retailing at the School, now held by Professor Malcolm P. McNair.

Lincoln Filene's ability in dealing with people was an important factor in the store's success. He inspired people and brought out the best in them. He believed that personnel are the key to successful management and relations with the public. His philosophy is outlined in his book *A Merchant's Horizon* (1924).

He believed strongly in research, in getting at facts on which to base intelligent judgment and purposeful action. He felt that industrial research would bring about better products which his store and others could make available to the public. And so, years ago, he urged the New England Council to engage in such research. This concept was comparatively new at the time and slow in making a start.

In 1929 in an address before the First Boston Conference on Distribution, which he encouraged throughout his life, he said: "The value of research in instructing us how to hold manpower is of the very first importance . . . the greatest force in competition of the future is intensive research within our own establishments to clarify our own thinking on the appreciation of our executives and the proper training of such executives to higher positions." On his initiative years ago the store organized a research department dealing with problems of the business, a novel project at the time.

In his aim to make merchandising more scientific, Lincoln Filene felt that exchange of information and ideas as to best practice among a group of representative stores in various cities would be desirable. In 1916 he broached the idea to the heads of eighteen of the nation's leading stores. They accepted the idea enthusiastically and set up the organization known as The Retail Research Association. Lincoln Filene was elected President and Chairman of the Executive Committee, which offices he held till 1943. In 1918 these stores formed the Associated Merchandising Corporation for the co-operative buying of much of their merchandise. Subsequently more stores were added to the group, including Harrods of London and the Myer Emporium, Ltd., in Melbourne, Australia. The volume of purchases has grown to over a billion dollars.

Both Filenes were born in Massachusetts of parents who came from Posen (then in Germany). Neither had the opportunity for a college education, as they were obligated to carry on the business of the small store established by their father in Salem, Massachusetts, and which moved to larger quarters in Boston. From that small beginning the brothers, aided by their colleagues, E.J. Frost, Louis E. Kirstein, H.D. Hodgkinson, and Samuel Seegal, built the store into the great institution it is today.

EA and Lincoln Filene were honored by many colleges for their activity in the public interest. EA received honorary LL.D. degrees from Lehigh University, Rollins College, and Tulane University. Lincoln received an honorary M.A. from Dartmouth and an LL.D. from Bates College, and was elected an honorary member of Phi Beta Kappa by the William and Mary College chapter.

Benjamin Horace Hibbard
1870-1955

11

Benjamin Horace Hibbard
1870-1955

by HENRY E. ERDMAN

BENJAMIN HORACE HIBBARD was born in Iowa on January 9, 1870. Because of his father's ill health, he soon had to operate the farm. During several winters he taught country school. It was not until March, 1895, that he enrolled at Iowa State College, a mature man of 25. During this 25-year span the marketing problem to which he was later to devote much time had been a burning issue. The index of prices farmers received dropped from 109 to 59 (1913=100), the Grange and the Farmers' Alliance rose and fell, and Iowa farmers were struggling to establish cooperative marketing.

Upon graduation in 1898, he accepted a position as instructor in mathematics at his Alma Mater. A year later he entered the University of Wisconsin for graduate work in economics and history. He received the Ph.D. degree in 1902. That fall he returned to Iowa State College to teach "economic science." With the exception of an eight-month leave for study in Germany in 1908, he remained at Iowa until called to Wisconsin in 1913.

In December of 1907, Hibbard presented a "working outline" for a course on "Agricultural Economics" at a round table of the American Economic Association. This included a section on "co-operative undertakings." That academic year his course in "Agricultural Economics" at Iowa State included the topics: co-operation, prices, transportation, marketing, and the relation of the state to agriculture.

Hibbard went to Wisconsin in January, 1913, as Professor of Agricultural Economics, a recognized specialist in marketing and cooperation. He was soon busy with teaching and with farmers' meetings concerned with marketing. He offered a new course titled

Journal of Marketing
Vol. XXIV No. 2, October, 1959
Reprinted by Permission

"Co-operation and Marketing," probably the first such in this country.

In the field of marketing he wrote an article for Bailey's Cyclopedia of Agriculture on "Co-operation in the Grain Elevator Business" (1909). At Wisconsin, usually with younger associates, he put out a series of agricultural experiment station bulletins on marketing and co-operation. These included: "Agricultural Co-operation" (1914); "Markets and Prices of Wisconsin Cheese" (1915, with Asher Hobson); "The Marketing of Wisconsin Butter" (1916, with Hobson); "Marketing Wisconsin Milk" (1917, with H.E. Erdman); and "Wisconsin Livestock Shipping Associations" (1920, with L.G. Foster and D. G. Davis).

Many of his numerous journal articles dealt with marketing, as did many public addresses. He was popular as a public speaker because his analytical approach was enlivened by his aptness at turning a phrase to drive home a point, and by his store of "that-reminds-me" stories used for the same purpose. His most widely known work on marketing is his *Marketing Agricultural Products* (1921).

Many of his writings dealt with a central cluster of questions farmers continued to raise: Why are spreads so wide between the farmer and the consumer: Who gets the money and for what services: What can the farmer do to improve matters?

Although Professor Hibbard was most widely known for his work in marketing, co-operation, and the history of farmers' movements, he wrote books and articles on such other aspects of the farm problem as tenancy, taxation, tariffs, and government control of prices. The most comprehensive in this general group are *A History of the Public Land Policies* (1924), and *Agricultural Economics* (1948).

Professor Hibbard died at Madison, Wisconsin, August 11, 1955, in his 86th year.

George Burton Hotchkiss
1884-1953

12

George Burton Hotchkiss 1884-1953

by D.B. LUCAS

GEORGE BURTON HOTCHKISS was born in Naugatuck, Connecticut, March 2, 1884. He spent his entire active career in teaching and writing, continuing to his death on March 28, 1953. All of his career was closely identified with his dedication to the art of writing and its applications to business. One year after his Yale A.B. (1905), and the year of his A.M. from Yale (1906), he won the student poetry prize with his contribution "The Birthright" (Perry Press). This was his first published work.

For two years he taught at Beloit College, and then came to New York University, where he remained. He taught English composition at the University Heights in addition to Business English and argumentation in the School of Commerce, Accounts, and Finance. Later he developed the business course of advertising copy, followed by the organization of the Department of Advertising and Marketing in 1915. As head of the new Department, he continued to expand the curriculum until, in 1928, he resigned the chairmanship to take a year's leave for scholarly study in England. He resumed the chairmanship upon the retirement of Professor Henry Elmer Agnew in 1943, a post he retained until 1950. That year he received an honorary Litt.D. from New York University and was made Professor Emeritus of Marketing.

While his pioneering vision and leadership in the teaching of advertising and marketing had great impact, his career may be held in better perspective by examining his writing. His first outstanding book, written in collaboration, was *Handbook of Business English* (Harper: 1914, 1916, 1917, 1920, 1945), followed by *Advanced Business Correspondence* (Harper: 1921, 1924, 1935, 1947).

Journal of Marketing
Vol. XXV No. 3, January, 1961
Reprinted by Permission

In collaboration with three other distinguished pioneers in the teaching of advertising, he wrote *Advertising, Its Principles and Practice*, published in 1915. The other three authors were Harry Tipper, a prominent advertising man, Dr. Harry L. Hollingworth, a noted psychologist, and Frank Alvah Parsons, outstanding commercial artist. The book was revised in 1919 and 1925 under a new title, *The Principles of Advertising*.

The next book, which he considered his greatest professional contribution, was *Advertising Copy* (Harper: 1924, 1936, 1949). During a period when the advertising business was beginning to attract the talents of gifted writers, *Advertising Copy* was a classic in its field, and for twenty-five years held a place on the *Printers' Ink* list of "The Best" advertising books. Never, before or since the publication of this book, has there been so much stress on the art of writing as it relates to expression in advertising.

After his sojourn in England, Professor Hotchkiss set about editing the treatise on which he had been doing extensive research in the British Museum, the Bodleian Library, and the Goldsmith's Library. It was published as *Wheeler's Treatise of Commerce* in 1931 by the New York University Press. This historical document stands as his most scholarly work.

Also, on the basis of his research abroad, Professor Hotchkiss published *Milestones of Marketing* (Macmillan: 1938). This was a history of the evolution of marketing methods with considerable emphasis on English trading activities.

His final full-length book was *An Outline of Advertising* (Macmillan: 1933, 1940, 1950). It has been used extensively as a college text for introductory courses in advertising. The frequency of his revisions of this book and others reflects his drive to keep revitalizing his guides for practitioners. To him the phrase, "the dynamics of advertising," had very real meaning.

While the major writings of Professor Hotchkiss reflect a rich, productive career, he managed to be prominent in many other activities. One of these was his service during World War I in the Bureau of Imports of the War Trade Board and as an associate of the Committee on Classification of Personnel in the Adjutant General's Office of the War Department, 1918-1919. This was the famous wartime personnel committee headed by the late Walter Dill Scott.

The New York University Chapter of Alpha Delta Sigma, national advertising fraternity, was established as the George Burton Hotchkiss Chapter in 1933. This chapter rapidly accumulated an unmatched host of the great leaders in the advertising business:

James D. Mooney, Ralph Starr Butler, William E. Robinson, George Gallup, Raymond Rubicam, Ben Duffy, Roy Larsen, Charles Mortimer, James Webb Young, and Lowell Thomas, to name just a few. Many of these men, in days before the teaching of marketing was so well recognized in colleges, said, "I don't know much about this organization, but if George Hotchkiss is connected with it, I accept!"

In a unique gesture *Advertising and Selling* magazine struck a Silver Medal and conferred it on Professor Hotchkiss in 1948 on the occasion of the Annual Advertising Awards "for distinguished services to advertising education." Then, in 1955, as regulations for posthumous awards permitted the recognition, Professor Hotchkiss was elected to the Advertising Hall of Fame.

Other professional activities included youthful experience as a reporter for the *New York Evening Sun*, and two years as a part-time copy writer for the George Batten Company. He served on several occasions as an expert witness, notably in 1943 when he testified at a hearing of the House Subcommittee investigating restrictions on brand names and newsprint. He was active in the American Marketing Association, and served as Vice President in 1937.

Always a great competitor and lover of sports, Professor Hotchkiss was an avid baseball fan and splendid golfer. He also kept a running chess game going in the Correspondence Chess League of America. He was deeply devoted to a wide range of interests, and always at the top of the list was his interest in his collection of rare books pertaining to business. His classroom lectures and his writings reflected the richness of his reading experience.

Leverett Samuel Lyon
1885-1959

13

Leverett Samuel Lyon
1885-1959

by N.H. ENGLE

LEVERETT SAMUEL LYON is one of the most distinguished members of the American Marketing Association. Educated in law and economics he has given liberally of himself as educator and executive. His eminently successful and varied career divides roughly into three eras: (1) teaching and writing in the midwest, largely at the University of Chicago and culminating in his service as Dean of the School of Commerce and Finance at Washington University in St. Louis from 1923 to 1925; (2) teaching, research, and administration with the Robert Brookings Graduate School of Economics and Government and the Brookings Institution in Washington, D.C., from 1925 to 1939; and (3) administrative work as Chief Executive Officer of the Chicago Association of Commerce from 1939 until 1954, when he became Chairman of the Executive Committee of the Association.

A pioneer in professional education for business at the university level, Leverett Lyon contributed substantially through his writing and his work with professional groups. Two of his early publications come to mind, *Our Economic Organization*, with L.C. Marshall, 1921—an excellent brief analysis of the American economic structure—and *Education for Business*, 1922. The latter work went through three editions, the last published in 1931.

His early interest in marketing is attested by his activities in organization work He participated in the formation of the National Association of Teachers of Marketing and Advertising which later merged with the American Marketing Society to become the American Marketing Association of today. Leverett Lyon was president in 1933 and active in the groundwork which eventuated in the formation of A.M.A.

Journal of Marketing
Vol. XXIII No. 4, April, 1959
Reprinted by Permission

It was during his years at Brookings that his greatest contributions to marketing emerged from his tireless research. Between 1925 and the inception of the New Deal such fundamental contributions to marketing literature as the following flowed from his pen: *Salesmen in Marketing Strategy*, 1926; *Hand-to-Mouth Buying*, 1929; *Some Trends in the Marketing of Canned Foods*, 1930; *Advertising Allowances*, 1932; and *The Economics of Free Deals*, 1933.

The free-wheeling experiments of the New Deal provided a challenging opportunity for the business researcher, which Leverett Lyon did not neglect. Through observation and actual participation he added to his wealth of economic knowledge. And he continued to share what he learned with all of us. Then in 1934 he published *The A.B.C. of the N.R.A.;* in 1935, *The National Recovery Administration—An Analysis and an Appraisal;* and in 1936, *The Economics of Open Price Systems* with V. Abramson. Perhaps his greatest contribution lies in the two-volume analysis of *Government and Economic Life*, published in 1939 and 1940 with the collaboration of Myron W. Watkins, Victor Abramson, and others of the Brookings family.

During his years in the nation's capital Leverett Lyon was inevitably drawn into government service in various capacities. He served, among other assignments, as U.S. delegate to the International Congress on Business Education in Amsterdam in 1929 and in London in 1932, and as deputy assistant administrator for trade practice policy for N.R.A. in 1934.

Returning to his native state in 1939 and taking on the heavy administrative responsibility of the Chicago Association of Commerce opened up new vistas to Leverett Lyon. The advent of World War II but added to his challenge. Those familiar with chamber-of-commerce activities generally cannot fail to discern the great contribution he made in this field. He continued to write, of course. The titles indicate the breadth of his research activity as well as the scope of his administrative duties. In 1944 appeared *Your Business and Postwar Adjustment,* followed by *Great Lakes—St. Lawrence Seaway and Power Project*, of which he was co-editor, *Prospects and Problems in Aviation*, 1945, and then *Modernizing a City Government*, 1954. He even found time to publish a book of verse called *Nothing but Nonsense.*

Leverett Lyon served the nation in two world wars. He was Editorial Assistant to the U.S. Food Administration during World War I and member of the Chicago Committee on National Defense during World War II. He also contributed to his state and community through membership in the Governor's Committee on Taxation (Illinois), the Chicago Planning Commission, the Advertising Board, Chicago, and the Chicago Civil Defense Commission.

Leverett Lyon has established a firm place in the affection of many a younger marketing man through his kindly encouragement and advice. He continues to serve as an inspiration and example to a host of former students and friends.

Editors' Afternote: Professor Engle wrote the following in the Fall of 1973:

    . . . Dr. Leverett Lyon died in the year in which my article was published. Mrs. Lyon wrote me that he had read the article and was particularly pleased that I had mentioned his interest and aid to young students.

Harold H. Maynard
1889-1957

14

Harold H. Maynard
1889-1957

by THEODORE N. BECKMAN

This brief biographical statement is not intended to record the full life and the many specific outstanding accomplishments of Professor Harold Howard Maynard. It is, instead, a brief appraisal of the significant contributions of a man who has labored diligently in the vineyards commonly cultivated by members of the marketing profession.

Dr. Maynard was born in Janesville, Iowa, May 31, 1889, and lived to March 13, 1957. His formal higher education resulted in an A.B. from Iowa State Teachers College in 1912, an A.M. from Harvard University in 1919, and a Ph.D. from the University of Iowa in 1922. A man of extremely curious bent, he never stopped learning. With him education was indeed a continuous process.

He came to The Ohio State University in 1923 where he remained all his life as a Professor of Business Organization and, since 1928, chairman of the Department. Prior to that he had taught at Vanderbilt University and the State College of Washington. In addition, he was a member of the summer faculties of the State University of Iowa, the University of Minnesota, Stanford University, the University of Pennsylvania, and the University of Denver. As a teacher in the classroom he thus exerted a lasting influence on many thousands of students, mostly on the advanced undergraduate and graduate levels. His teaching extended, however, beyond the classroom to the speaker's platform on many hundreds of occasions, and the conference rooms of a number of leading business corporations.

In the area of research and writing, Dr. Maynard's first contribution was the published form of his doctoral dissertation, *Marketing*

Journal of Marketing
Vol. XXIII No. 4, April, 1959
Reprinted by Permission

Northwestern Apples (1923). Like most of the writings in the field in those early days, it was agricultural-marketing oriented. This is evidenced by such books as *Reducing the Cost of Food Distribution* (1913) published by the American Academy of Political and Social Science; L.D.H. Weld's *The Marketing of Farm Products* (1916); Edwin G. Nourse's *The Chicago Produce Market* (1918); and B. H. Hibbard's *Marketing Agricultural Products* (1921).

Whether and to what extent such orientation is to be ascribed to the more agrarian character of our economy at that time, the influences of the first teachers of marketing, the sheer inertia in the direction first taken, the rural environment or background of the early writers on the subject, the stirrings caused by the co-operative movement, or by other factors, poses an interesting subject of inquiry for the historically minded student of marketing.

In the first opus, Dr. Maynard's effort, in line with the needs and standards of the time, was chiefly descriptive, being concerned primarily with methods of marketing specific farm products and how to improve them. The approach was definitely functional, following the tracings outlined by Paul Cherington a few years before. Emphasis was on factual information obtained first-hand, and only incidentally was there a search for cause-and-effect relationships.

This characterization is important for two reasons. First, it means that the merit of his first work is to be judged in the light of the intellectual climate and requirements then prevailing rather than by present-day standards. Second, just as a psychiatrist looks at early experiences of an individual for a possible explanation of later developments, so may the early writings of an author, as in this case, provide a clue to some of his later works and perhaps furnish a better insight into the nature of subsequent contributions.

Dr. Maynard progressed substantially and steadily in his thinking on marketing subjects. More and more emphasis was placed by him on quantitative expression, cause-and-effect relationships, principles, theory (without necessarily labeling it as such), and the art of problem-solving and decision-making. Yet all along he continued to stress the importance of facts, the need for gathering information directly from the business concerns, and for basic knowledge bearing on the *what* and *how.*

This is reflected in his contributions as co-author of *An Introduction to Business Management* (1st edition in 1925 and 4th edition in 1951); *Principles of Marketing* (1st edition in 1927 and 6th edition in 1957); *Sales Management* (1st edition in 1940 and 3rd edition in 1957); and the numerous other materials which he authored or co-authored. Consider especially his numerous examples used to illustrate and fortify more general expression of method, practice, principle, or theory.

With his writings and inspiration to co-workers he helped to provide necessary materials for some of the basic courses in marketing taught at many colleges and universities, and continued to add to such literature until the end. In recognition of such important contributions to the development of marketing literature and a better understanding and appreciation of the marketing process he was entered in 1953 in the Hall of Fame in Distribution by the Boston Conference on Distribution.

Special notice must be taken of Professor Maynard's leadership in the broad activities of the field of marketing. From the very beginning he served as a member of the National Association of Marketing Teachers and the American Marketing Association. In both of these organizations he served variously as a member of committees, as a member of the Board of Directors, and as President; and to both organizations he gave of his energy and talent unstintingly. This kind of leadership extended beyond academic and professional marketing circles to a number of business organizations such as the Advertising Club and the Sales Executives Club. He was equally prominent and active in civic affairs.

Most of the things written up to this point deal with external manifestations of the man observable to all willing to make the effort. There were, however, certain facets of Dr. Maynard's personality that are probably known only to those who like the author of this statement, were privileged to work with him as a colleague and co-author for many years. Throughout World War II he labored unceasingly as chairman of a local rationing board, and undertaking that required all spare time from regular duties and responsibilities. Most important, he took a keen and extremely sympathetic interest in students, especially on the graduate level, and followed their paths through life's journey for many years, always with the central objective of improving their lot and speeding their advancement.

From the foregoing it is apparent that Professor Maynard was deeply devoted to his calling. He was an inspiring teacher and a forceful leader in the field of marketing. He was dedicated to the scholarship that would tend to advance the science of marketing. He was a humanitarian, a friendly counselor, and a most worthy colleague.

Edwin Griswold Nourse
1883-

15

Edwin Griswold Nourse 1883-

by E.T. GRETHER

The life and writings of Edwin G. Nourse clearly demonstrate the relative youthfulness of the field of marketing as an academic study and discipline. Here, as in other instances in this biographical series, is a man who is still contributing actively to scientific literature and to public policy, even though he was a pioneer author and scholar in the field of marketing.

The Chicago Produce Market which appeared in 1918 was the published form of Dr. Nourse's doctoral dissertation written under Professor J. Laurence Laughlin at the University of Chicago in 1914-15, and later revised under the direction of the then Assistant Professor Melvin T. Copeland of the Harvard Graduate School of Business Administration. Dr. Nourse recounted at the University of Illinois Symposium in the fall of 1955, when he received the Paul D. Converse Award, that it was somewhat of a shock at the University of Chicago when he suggested making this empirical marketing study for his doctoral dissertation. But he had been a farm boy during the period when farmers and urban consumers felt very strongly that certain monopolistic and Machiavellian influences were working against them in American markets. *The Chicago Produce Market* was an institutional exploration into the workings of one aspect of the mysterious mechanism and forces operating between farmers and city consumers in one important market. At the same time a number of other pioneering studies of agricultural marketing were under way, including L.D.H. Weld, *The Marketing of Farm Products* (1916).

When the youthful Edwin G. Nourse undertook this market investigation instead of the one in the field of money and credit

Journal of Marketing
Vol. XXII No. 4, April, 1958
Reprinted by Permission

that had been anticipated, because of his position as assistant to Professor Laughlin, he foreshadowed a pattern of interest and analysis that has run throughout his entire career. To him the market was not a passive or neutral factor in the price-making process but, by its structure and practices, went far to determine which demands were brought in touch with which sources of supply. Markets and marketeers therefore were dynamic forces in activating and guiding consumer or user demands and in discovering, stimulating, and aiding suppliers. This thesis was explicitly developed in an article "Normal Price as a Market Concept," *Quarterly Journal of Economics*, August, 1919.

Dr. Nourse's basic interests and inquiring mind led him for years into a number of careful investigations in the field of agricultural marketing. Typical products of these inquiries were: *The Legal Status of Agricultural Cooperation* (1927), and *The Cooperative Marketing of Livestock* (with J.G. Knapp, 1931). But he was equally interested in exploring industrial production, marketing, and pricing. The results of these explorations appeared in such volumes as *America's Capacity to Produce* (with associates, 1934); *Industrial Price Policies and Economic Progress* (with H.B. Drury, 1938); and *Price Making in a Democracy* (1944). In the latter two instances, as well as in other studies, such as *Marketing Agreements under the Agricultural Adjustment Administration* (1935) and *Three Years of the Agricultural Adjustment Administration* (with J.S. Davis and J.D. Black, 1937), he was reporting also upon the character and effects of private and governmental intrusions upon the guiding role of free markets.

These studies and experiences, and numerous others, provided excellent background for Dr. Nourse when he became the first Chairman of the Council of Economic Advisers in the Executive Offices of the President of the United States in 1946 under the Employment Act of 1946. In accordance with his background and experience he persistently stressed the importance of price or market adjustments as a means of attaining stability and promoting the growth of the economy no less than the complementary over-all influences of fiscal and monetary measures.

Space cannot be taken here to review in full Dr. Nourse's contributions to scholarship, to academic instruction, and to private and public policy. An incomplete bibliography records that he is the author of some 150 publications (excluding governmental reports) ranging all the way from an article "Has a Pig More Sense than a Sophomore?," *Country Gentleman*, December 27, 1924, to his book *Economics in the Public Service* (1953). In the latter volume he interpreted his experience as Chairman of the Council of Economic Advisers in Washington. Early in his career Dr. Nourse held academic appointments at the University of Pennsylvannia, University of South Dakota, the University of Arkansas, and Iowa State College. Just prior to his appointment as Chairman of the Council of Economic Advisers by President Harry S. Truman in 1946, he was the Vice-President of the Brookings Institution. He has received the highest recognition that professional associations can bestow, including the Presidency of the American Economic Association (1942), of the American Farm Association (1924), and Chairmanship of the Social Science Research Council.

The dominant factor that gave form and substance to the career and contributions of Edwin Griswold Nourse has been the desire to understand and explain the workings of our price and market system. Few men, if any, have made greater contributions to such an understanding. But Dr. Nourse also has had the unusual opportunity of making direct applications in the public service at the highest level of influence of his knowledge, wisdom, and high standards of professionsl performance.

Editors' Afternote: Edwin G. Nourse continues to be a scholar in the public service. At the age of 90 he is completing a book that will be his testament for present and future Americans on what he has learned in his long career as an economist and social scientist. He maintains an office provided to him by the Brookings Institution. He has the intellectual zest of a young man and he looks ever forward in the light of his deep knowledge of the past.

Paul Henry Nystrom
1878-1969

16

Paul Henry Nystrom
1878-1969

by DELBERT J. DUNCAN

Paul H. Nystrom "retired" from Columbia University in 1950 and as president of the Limited Price Variety Stores Association a few years later. But as his many friends well know, such a staunch and sturdy pioneer in the field of marketing in general and in retailing in particular will never actually retire. His keen and active mind, sharpened by a strong interest in current business developments, has brought intellectual stimulation to many thousands of students and businessmen. This stimulation has generated a high degree of inquiry within himself and resulted in numerous valuable contributions to our marketing literature.

Dr. Nystrom's first pioneering effort in the field of distribution was *Retail Selling and Store Management*, published in 1913. Although lacking in factual data and comprehensiveness measured by today's standards, it provided valuable information for instructional and managerial purposes in a field where organized knowledge was very limited. The first edition of *Economics of Retailing* followed in 1915 and by its third edition in 1930 had grown into a two-volume "bible of retailing." Between these editions he authored *Economics of Fashion* (1928) and the *Economics of Consumption* (1929). By 1930 interest in retailing courses in colleges and universities was becoming quite pronounced, and operators of retail stores were searching for "principles" to guide their efforts into the most profitable channels. Awareness of this fact led Dr. Nystrom to continue his research efforts and in 1932 *Fashion Merchandising* was published. In these later volumes especially he recognized the importance of integrating theory and practice, and his foresight and judgment have been demonstrated to a convincing

Professor Duncan revised this sketch which originally appeared in Vol. XXI No. 4, April, 1957 of the Journal of Marketing.

degree by developments in recent years. His *Retail Store Operation* (1937) and his editorship of the *Marketing Handbook* (1948) constituted his latest efforts in the textbook field.

But Dr. Nystrom's contributions to the advancement of marketing extend far beyond his formalized writings. His impressive career includes teaching and research responsibilities at the universities of Wisconsin and Minnesota and at Columbia University. While at the latter institution, he served as president of the Limited Price Variety Stores Association from 1933 to 1955 and also as president of the Sales Executives Club of New York at two different times, 1937-38 and 1940-45. Previously, he had been a director of the Retail Research Association and the Associated Merchandising Corporation. These responsibilities, plus his teaching obligations, however, did not prevent him from actively participating in marketing organizations or from assisting the federal government in the areas of his competency. He made important contributions in both fields.

As president of the American Marketing Society in 1934 and editor of its *American Marketing Journal* during 1935-36, Dr. Nystrom did much to strengthen that organization as a prelude to its merger in 1937 with the National Association of Marketing Teachers to form the American Marketing Association.

His governmental service was extensive and varied. It included, for example, such diverse responsibilities as the acting chairmanship of the National Retail Code Authority under the National Recovery Administration and chairman of the Federal Board of Vocational Education at two different periods. His long and keen interest in vocational education caused him to champion the benefits of distributive education before governmental groups and contributed to the passage of the George-Deen Act in 1936.

These activities and others brought Dr. Nystrom widespread recognition and numerous honors. Among these were the Paul D. Converse Award at the University of Illinois in 1949, the honorary degree of LL.D. by The Ohio State University in 1950, and the Charles C. Parlin Award by the American Marketing Association in 1952. The King of Sweden conferred upon him the Decorated Order North Star 1st Class in 1950.

As one reviews the distinguished career of this remarkable man he is impressed with the broad interests, the significant accomplishments, and the enormous vitality he demonstrated in all of his undertakings. Dr. Nystrom's broad training and experience enabled him to combine effectively the "theories" of the classroom and the policies and practices of marketing institutions. He left an indelible impression upon his students.

The high esteem in which Paul H. Nystrom is held by his former students and university associates as well as by businessmen and government officials who knew him is probably the best tribute that may be paid this early leader in the marketing field. Yet his pioneering writings, his energetic search for improvements in our marketing practices and his critical appraisal of them in the light of changing conditions, will continue to inspire students of marketing for years to come.

Charles Coolidge Parlin
1872-1942

17

Charles Coolidge Parlin
1872-1942

by WROE ALDERSON

The first full-fledged market research organization in the United States was that established by the Curtis Publishing Company in 1911. The head of this organization for its first 27 years was Charles Coolidge Parlin.

Mr. Parlin was certainly one of the earliest pioneers in the infant science of marketing and unquestionably the first to apply orderly fact finding to problems in the field of advertising. He was born in the small village of Broadhead, Wisconsin, in 1872. His father, who was a buyer and shipper of farm produce, died when the boy was eight years old. He obtained a degree at the University of Wisconsin, financing his college education partly through his own efforts. While there, he was especially active in debating and public speaking. He cherished the ambition of entering law, but became a school teacher instead because of the need to begin earning a living immediately upon graduation.

His invitation from Curtis to undertake a new type of activity in business came when he was thirty-eight years old and serving as a high school principal in Wisconsin. The inspiration for this fact-finding approach to advertising problems and the nomination of Mr. Parlin to head it was the inspiration of Stanley Latshaw, one of Mr. Parlin's former high school students.

He began to make history at once in his new field of endeavor with the first thoroughgoing marketing studies of entire industries that had ever been made. The first of these were his monumental study of the farm implement market published in 1911 and his department store study published in four volumes in 1912. Mr. Parlin was one of the first to be concerned about the classification

Journal of Marketing
Vol. XXI No. 1, July, 1956
Reprinted by Permission

of goods according to their marketing characteristics and to provide factual evidence concerning the distinction between shopping goods and convenience goods. A third major study was that of the young automobile industry published in 1914, which was very influential in shaping the marketing and advertising policies of this industry.

Mr. Parlin undertook a census of distribution in 1920, nine years before the first national census of distribution was made by the Department of Commerce. In this study, he analyzed all cities of over 50,000 population and about 35 minor cities, estimating their trading population and volume of business.

He developed many concepts and techniques which, with refinements, are still in use today. Among these were the use of a buying-power index, city marketing maps reflecting purchasing power by neighborhoods, the study of consumer attitudes and buying habits through house-to-house surveys, and methods for evaluating magazine circulations.

Up to the day of his retirement, he was very ingenious in devising new methods of obtaining market information, one of the last studies that he directed being his "Dry Waste Survey" in which he established some important facts concerning patterns of food consumption by collecting and sorting discarded cartons, cans, and bottles from a representative sample of families. Throughout his career in marketing, Mr. Parlin was in great demand as a public speaker and exerted a significant influence on the development of both advertising and marketing research. He was honered posthumously in both fields by election to the Advertising Hall of Fame in 1953 and by the establishment of the Charles Coolidge Parlin Memorial Award by the Philadelphia Chapter of the American Association in 1945. His counsel was often sought by both government and business groups. For example, he served as a member of a permanent advisory committee on the marketing studies of the Department of Commerce when Herbert Hoover was Secretary. He represented the position of business and the advertising fraternity most effectively during the protracted hearings on grade labeling before a senatorial committee.

Outside his active business career, Mr. Parlin devoted himself to his family and his church and in later years to world travel. Mr. Parlin and all four children were musically gifted and the Parlin family orchestra was well known for some years in Germantown. Both of his sons have realized their father's ambition in making successful careers as lawyers.

With only limited formal training in either economics or statistics, Mr. Parlin developed a shrewd and consistent economic philosophy and great practical skill as a statistician.

He was a pioneer not only in marketing research but in the increasing orientation of management as a whole toward the market. Year after year, his countless speeches to business groups closed with the ringing declaration, "the consumer is king!"

Stanley B. Resor
1879-1962

18

Stanley B. Resor
1879-1962

by LAURENCE WILE JACOBS

Stanley Burnet Resor was once described as "one of the least articulate men alive" and yet he was the driving force which caused the greatness of the J. Walter Thompson Advertising Agency.

At his graduation from Yale in 1901, the 22 year old Resor received the James Gordon Bennett prize in Economics which carried with it a $60 award. During his Yale years he helped to support himself financially by tutoring Latin which gave him the inspiration to become a teacher. His summers were spent learning lessons in consumer motivation that he would carry forth into the advertising world. This knowledge was achieved by selling a history of the Bible door-to-door throughout Southern Ohio and by distributing samples of Pearl Soap at factory gates.

Armed with his academic knowledge of language and economics and his practical insights into customer motivation, Stanley Resor concluded to forego a teaching career. He also decided against entering the failing family stove business and went to seek a job in his native Cincinnati. This was a somewhat difficult task in that most self-made businessmen of the era were rather suspicious of college graduates in general and eastern school products in particular. After much searching he finally took a job for $5 a week with a bank. Two years later he left the bank to work as a shipping clerk with the Lodge and Shipley Tool Company.

The next year, 1904, Stanley Resor entered the field of advertising with Procter and Collier, job printers and house advertising

This sketch was specially written for this volume in lieu of the one appearing in Vol. XXV No. 6, October, 1961 issue of the Journal of Marketing.

agency for Procter and Gamble. Also employed at Procter and Collier were his brother Walter and a copywriter named Helen Lansdowne. After four years of successes his efforts were noticed by Charles E. Raymond, who was the head of J. Walter Thompson's Chicago office. Raymond asked Stanley and his brother to head the new Thompson Cincinnati office. Like executives in most small agencies, the Resor brothers did everything from copywriting to soliciting accounts.

In 1912 Stanley and Walter were moved, Walter to the Boston office, which he headed until his death in 1940, and Stanley to the New York office. It was in 1916 that the 69 years old James Walter Thompson sold his 48-year-old agency to Stanley Resor and Charles Raymond for $500,000 (mostly borrowed). J. Walter was convinced that the advertising business had peaked out and most of Resor's friends gave the company less than a year before bankruptcy. Later in the year retiring Raymond sold his holdings to James Webb Young, head of the Cincinnati office and Henry Stanton, an associate of Young's in Cincinnati. Along with Helen Lansdowne who had previously joined the New York office, they became the "Cincinnati Group."

In 1916 the Thompson Agency had 177 employees in five offices (New York, Chicago, Cincinnati, Detroit, and Boston) and served about 300 clients with billings of about 3 million dollars. Resor's first task was to cut the client list to 80 profitable accounts. From this point on the growth (except in 1931 and 1932) was steady but far from slow.

Selected years	Total Billings (in Millions)
1916	3.2
1925	18
1930	38
1932	30
1935	36
1945	73
1955	231

The year after becoming head of the J. Walter Thompson Company, 38-year-old Stanley Resor married Helen Lansdowne. Although she was not thereafter on the payroll, Helen made large contributions to the creative strategy of the Thompson Group.

Working together, Stanley with his talent for the practical and Helen with her flair for the dramatic, the Resors made an unbeatable pair. It seems only natural that the practical and the dramatic should find their outlet in testimonial type advertising. While testimonial advertising was not invented by the Thompson Agency, the Resors certainly used it to full advantage as early as 1924 with the Pond's Cleansing and Vanishing Cream account. With this combination of Helen's drive and Stanley's business judgement, it is little wonder that the J. Walter Thompson Agency was destined for greatness.

Advertising as a selling tool rather than as a form of showmanship a la P.T. Barnum and the patent medicine men was Resor's philosophy. He believed that advertising is more than copy and art but is based upon a careful study of business problems. Thoroughness, not copy brilliance, was the credo of the Thompson Group under Resor's leadership and the path to thoroughness is research and more research. The output of the agency stressed "reason-why" copy based upon this research rather than seeking the stroke of creative genius which characterized many other agencies.

As a great admirer of facts, Resor was a major force in changing advertising from pure art to an art form based upon research and the scientific method. This quest for facts carried beyond the walls of the agency and Stanley became instrumental in the formation and support of the Audit Bureau of Circulation, the Outdoor Advertising Bureau, and the Advertising Research Foundation.

Under his leadership the Thompson Agency refused to make any speculative presentations to prospective clients. ("This is what we will do for you.") Resor was against this common practice because the prospective agency could not know all of the marketing facts and therefore was not in a position to create the same quality ads as in an established agency-client relationship.

Resor used facts to predict human behavior which, he felt, could be anticipated at least on a mass basis. Resor wrote in 1927, "Advertising is based on a study of habit," so using a combination of common sense and imagination he conducted empirical studies. These in turn formed the basis of advertisements. As Resor once phrased it, ". . .The work of advertising is first to locate and analyze markets and secondly to influence the people who constitute those markets."

This emphasis upon the fact gathering gave rise to the famous "Thompson T Square".

What are we selling
To Whom are we selling
Where are we selling
When are we selling
How are we selling

Within the agency, the structure encouraged no dominant luminaries. Resor sought consensus rather than individual opinion and believed that advertising is the product of many people working together toward a common purpose. The best work, he felt, remains anonymous.

Resor practiced an "open-door" policy as did his Thompson associates. He preferred the drift-in, drift-out type of meetings to the more formal ones. He also followed the philosophy that Juniors did not report to Seniors. Rather it was the function of the Seniors to "backstop" the Juniors in the service of clients.

As early as 1917 Resor was making his ethical feelings known in the advertising industry for in that year, as one of the founders of the American Association of Advertising Agencies, he committed his agency to the high standards of professionalism of the 4A's. He was described by *Fortune* in 1947 as follows:

Stanley Resor has over the years come to be nothing less than the personification of Ethics. It has been his belief that advertising must become more and more a profession . . . and the advertising man more a subscriber to a self-imposed code of conduct.

Resor's efforts in making the advertising industry more ethically responsible were recognized a year later when he was awarded the advertising industry's Gold Medal Award for "distinguished service."

Resor had a dream about the ultimate destiny of Advertising. He viewed advertising as more than large-scale selling to command markets for large-scale manufacturers. He dreamed that someday advertising would produce a world of peace and understanding. In his acceptance speech of the Gold Medal Award for distinguished service Resor said, "In the modern world, we have available all the means of communication. It would be ironic if we do not use them to disseminate the truth." Advertising, to Resor, has a major impact on the fulfillment of human wants and needs by delivering not only products but attitudes. Advertising is an educational force which should be used for good.

In its feature article in 1947, *Fortune* described Resor:

At sixty-eight, Mr. Resor is as indomitable in the affairs of the agency he has made great as ever he was in the beginning. Under his white hair his face shows the color and expression of a healthy and happy man, obviously determined to run the J. Walter Thompson Co. forever.

Stanley Resor continued to serve as president until 1955 when at age 76 he became chairman of the board. He served in this capacity until 1961.

Fortune continues its description:

Whereas the Advertising business is supposed to be shot through with a cynical callousness toward truth and beauty, the top man of the top U. S. agency believes totally in the power and goodness of advertising, the problems of war and peace, religion, morality, a new humanity of man toward man—all are susceptible, as Stanley Resor sees it to the power of advertising properly employed.

Stanley Resor died on Oct. 29, 1962. He was 83.

Clarence Saunders
1881-1953

19

Clarence Saunders
1881-1953

by PERSIS EMMETT ROCKWOOD

Clarence Saunders, pioneer of the supermarket and other marketing innovations, was born in Amherst County, Virginia, on August 9, 1881.[1] At age nineteen he became a salesman for the Hurst-Boillin wholesale grocery firm in Clarksville, Tennessee, where his special abilities began to appear. It is said that his salary doubled quickly, and he was moved to Memphis, which remained his home and headquarters.

He enhanced his success as a grocery salesman by offering suggestions to his retailer customers for improving the efficiency of their operations. He saw the importance of scale economies in the industry and concentrated on obtaining volume business. He helped a group of grocers form United Stores, Inc., and continued to sell to the chain. Eager to operate independently, he established in 1915 his own wholesale business with $23,000 assistance from backers. In a year or so the business grew to a volume of two million dollars. But Saunders' concern with volume and competitive price overshadowed his concern for costs, and anticipated profits were absent.

In 1916, he opened the first Piggly Wiggly store in Memphis, at 79 Jefferson Street. The store layout was unique. Customers passed through a turnstile; followed a maze of aisles lined with merchandise; served themselves from the shelves, placing purchases in a basket; paid a cashier; and exited through another turnstile. The stores caught the public fancy. There were twenty-five stores by 1917 and over 1,200 by 1922, 650 owned by Saunders' Piggly Wiggly Stores, Inc. The remainder were independently owned, and the owners paid a royalty for use of the patented method of

This sketch was specially written for this volume. Mr. Saunders was not featured in the "Pioneers in Marketing" series.

operation. A factory manufactured store equipment. Saunders patented his turnstile and wrote store operator's manuals. In seven years his business was worth nearly a hundred million dollars.

The episode that made Saunders the last of the men to corner the stock market began in November, 1922, when several small grocery companies in the Northeast failed. They were independent firms which had bought use of the name and leased patented equipment for the stores from Saunders. Some unidentified speculators saw an opportunity in the situation to capitalize on the illusion that the Piggly Wiggly organization might fail, and they sold Piggly stock short, driving the price down from around 50 to 39. To support the stock and protect his investment, Saunders borrowed about ten million dollars from southern bankers and bought Piggly Wiggly shares. He marshaled a number of Wall Street brokers to manage the endeavor, including Jesse L. Livermore. Saunders bought 30,000 shares in one day and a total of 105,000 within the week.

When the stock was selling at 70 in February, 1923, in a move to relieve his financial extension while keeping his shares out of the hands of short sellers, he advertised 50,000 shares for sale to the public at 55, payment to be in installments of twenty-five dollars down and three quarterly payments of ten dollars each. Stock certificates would be delivered upon completion of payment.

In March, Saunders was reported to have owned or controlled through installment sales all but about 1,128 of the 200,000 shares outstanding. Whether or not the figure is accurate, he had a corner. On March 20, Saunders demanded delivery, knowing that was impossible within the 24-hour interval prescribed by the rules of the New York Stock Exchange. The price rose to 124 as those who had sold short attempted to cover their commitments. Saunders anticipated defeat of his adversaries. However, the Exchange, following anxious observation of events, suspended trading in the stock and granted extension of the delivery period to five days. Then the Exchange announced that Piggly Wiggly was removed from its trading list. Thus, Saunders found himself heavily in debt and the owner of a large quantity of high-priced stock. After settling part of the loans, attempts to sell the stock to repay the remaining bank loans failed. He sold some of his stores, those in Chicago, Denver, and Kansas City. But he was forced out of the presidency of his company and then into bankruptcy.

Within the next decade Saunders made three attempts to recoup his fortune in diverse innovative enterprises. The first was a chain of stores under the name Clarence Saunders, Sole Owner of My Name,

Stores. Again he opened a multiplicity of stores; but again he failed, this time in 1931, in the depth of the depression. After the bankruptcy there were still more than a hundred of the stores.

What remains an interesting and insightful merchandising and technical innovation was developed next. In 1935, Saunders formed the Keedoozle Corporation to merchandise groceries by means of an original patented system. Robert A. Black, formerly a St. Louis merchandiser, and Lee Saunders, a son of Clarence, were the other incorporators. The Keedoozle (key does all) store contained samples of merchandise, up to 1,200 items or more displayed behind glass with the items classified and each one priced. The customer was given a numbered "key," a rod about nine inches long with a knot on the end. The key was inserted in slots in the glass cases, a slot for each item. As merchandise was selected with the key, the items were registered electrically by an adding machine at the conveyor belt. When all purchases were made the key was inserted in a master keyhole which activated the adding machine to register the total. The items selected from the inventory descended by a gravity chute behind the stock shelves to a conveyor belt which moved them to the front of the store. After paying his bill, the customer received his groceries in a basket from a numbered booth corresponding to the number of the key.

A small store could be operated by two people. Saunders claimed that it would accommodate up to ten times as many shoppers as the average store. Shrinkage, spoilage, and theft of merchandise would be reduced to a minimum. It was Saunders' plan to own two dozen stores in Memphis, and to grant franchises for use of the name and the system. The franchise price would be one-half of one percent of sales. It was planned to sell the machinery to independent operators.

After numerous delays the doors of the first Keedoozle opened on May 15, 1937, at 1624-28 Union Street, Memphis. The mechanics of the operation introduced some problems of inaccuracy and expense. A variety of chutes was required to handle the diverse product packages. Some errors in filling orders occurred, about two percent by Saunders' estimate. By March, 1938, meat and other products were handled manually instead of automatically, and gradually a majority of the handling became manual.

Another change was made. A different type of key was introduced. It resembled a pistol and contained a strip of paper on which the name and price of everything purchased was registered. Also, provision was made for customers to converse with the butcher. A wider line of goods including drugs and delicatessen items was contemplated. Cost of the equipment after the changes was reduced from $15,000 to $5,000.

Expansion came soon. In October, 1938, it was announced that improved electrical delivery equipment would be installed in the store on Union Street and a second store opened at Third and Jefferson, Memphis, two blocks from the site of his first Piggly Wiggly store. The new store was scheduled to carry variety lines as well as food. It had a parking space across the street.

The Union store was closed in late October, 1939, and in December, 1940, the Third and Jefferson unit was closed. At the time tax liens were filed: personal income taxes for 1936-38, $23,794.61, were claimed against Saunders and $1,092.30 against the Keedoozle Corporation. In January, 1941, some of the Keedoozle assets were sold to satisfy the liens. There were plans to open a store in Chicago and tentative plans for others in Texas and in Los Angeles.

From the time the Keedoozle stores closed in December, 1941, Saunders continued to work on his automatic system to have it perfected and ready for operation when the war ended. Awaiting planned grocery activity at war's end, about 1943 he designed a little wagon and push cart and planned to make them, operating as the S.S. (Saunders Special) Sales Co. The wagon had a removable tongue to permit use of the vehicle as a coaster, steered as is an automobile. The push cart was to be used to transport groceries and other purchases from store to home and as a baby buggy. He hoped to avoid wartime materials restrictions in manufacture by using scrap lumber and a few nails.

The last original development and an attempt to regain his fortune was the Foodelectric store. He planned to embark on the venture, a simplification and improvement of the Keedoozle store, in 1953. The customer was to use a "key" to obtain each item of merchandise from its enclosed show case. The key contained an "adding machine" in a 3 by 1¼ inch space with four rows of figures. When the key was fitted into a slot, the price of the item selected was registered in the adding machine by means of nine teeth in the receptacle. The customer carried his purchases to the cashier and paid his bill. The conveyor, the source of much trouble in the Keedoozle, was eliminated. Four people could operate a store with a million dollars' volume annually, it was estimated. Saunders announced that nothing in the Foodelectric store would be sold below cost and that prices would average ten percent less than any other merchandiser charged. Saunders planned to incorporate his venture, own and operate the stores in Memphis, and franchise stores in other cities for a quarter of one percent of sales.

Throughout his colorful merchandising career, Clarence Saunders was a figure the public found interesting, an exuberant and daring gladiator in business life. He was gifted with an intuitive understanding of selling and promotion. He was willing to accept high business risks. He was confident or despairing as fortune fluctuated, with an ever-resilient toughness of spirit. He was known widely as a generous man. His strong sense of honorable business conduct and his trusting nature sometimes made him prey to unworthy schemes. His flair for promotion may account for his intense interest in Tennessee politics, an interest once directed to the election of Austin Peay as governor over the powerful Ed Crump. His determination never faltered. At the time of his death in October, 1953, he was planning to open another Foodelectric Store.

Clarence Saunders left an enduring mark on Memphis. The three beautiful homes he built remain landmarks. The first became the University Club. The second, a pink Georgia marble and granite mansion known as the Pink Palace, was to become the Memphis Museum of Natural History and Industrial Arts and also the Little Theater. Annswood, a country estate, was auctioned to baseball star Bill Terry. The private golf course he built eventually was developed as Chickasaw Gardens residential subdivision.

Two sons followed their father's occupational interest by becoming entrepreneurs in the food and automatic vending industries. That family business interest has now extended to the third generation.

[1] This account was drawn mostly from local newspaper accounts. Sources on the life of Clarence Saunders are limited and contradictory in some details. Additional information about his effort to corner the market is found in John Brooks, *Business Adventures* (N.Y.: Weybright and Talley, 1969) pp. 224--48. Another general source is Shields McIlwaine, *Memphis: Down to Dixie* (N.Y.: E.P. Dutton, 1948), pp. 268–79.

Walter Dill Scott
1869-1955

20

Walter Dill Scott
1869-1955

by C.H. SANDAGE

Walter Dill Scott was a true pioneer in advertising and marketing. His great contribution was that of testing some of the basic theories and tenets of psychology and translating them into a language that could be understood and used by advertising men.

Dr. Scott was born in Cooksville, Inninois, May 1, 1869. His formal education was both diversified and extensive. He was graduated from Illinois State Normal University in 1891, received his A.B. from Northwestern in 1895, was graduated from McCormick Theological Seminary in 1898, and received his Ph.D. in psychology from the University of Leipzig in 1900. He later received honary degrees from such schools as Cornell and Southern California.

The productive life of Dr. Scott can perhaps be classified into three main categories: (1) educator, researcher, writer; (2) business consultant and army service; and (3) administrator.

Marketing men have been influenced primarily by Scott's work as an educator, researcher, and writer. He was a member of the teaching and research faculty of Northwestern University from 1901 to 1920. During that time he served as director of the psychology laboratory at the university and wrote extensively. His first important work of direct concern to advertising people was his *Theory of Advertising*,published in 1903. This work resulted from a series of articles written at the behest of members of the Agate Club of Chicago and originally carried in *Mahin's Magazine*. The articles and book dealt with psychological principles of significance to advertisers, but the term "psychology" was left out of the title in deference to purists who might be offended by having psychology associated with advertising and selling.

Journal of Marketing
Vol. XXV No. 5, July, 1961
Reprinted by Permission

It was not until 1908 that Scott brought the terms "psychology" and "advertising" together in a major publication. This was his *Psychology of Advertising* book which was destined to influence the thinking of vast numbers of both educators and practitioners. Scott kept this book active through four editions (the fourth edition published in 1921).

Other important publications of Scott included: *Psychology of Public Speaking*, 1907; *Influencing Men in Business*, 1911; *Psychology of Advertising Theory and Practice*, 1921; *Science and Common Sense in Working with Men*, 1921; and *Personnel Management*, 1923.

The titles of Scott's publications indicate a breadth of interests, but all are concerned with the psychological foundations on which effective communication of impressions and ideas are based. His primary concepts are still in vogue even though some of them are now expressed in more sophisticated language. He did not use the term "model" in his writings, but he clearly outlined the elements of a communications model to guide advertisers in their search for entry into the minds and emotions of people.

During World War I Scott served as director of the Commission on Classification of Personnel in the U.S. Army. He was awarded the Distinguished Service Medal for "devising, installing, and supervising the personnel system in the Army." He also served as a Colonel in the Army, 1918-19.

Scott spent a year before the war 1916-17, as Director of the Bureau of Salesmanship Research at Carnegie Institute of Technology. Immediately after the war he organized and served as President (1919-21) of the Scott Company which functioned as consultants and engineers in industrial personnel.

In 1920 he was named President of Northwestern University and served in that capacity until his retirement in 1939. He died in 1955.

Certainly the field of advertising owes much to Walter Dill Scott. He was a keen student of human nature, well-trained in psychological theory, highly capable of applying his theories to the solution of practical problems, and successful in influencing many advertisers to follow his counsel. He generously shared his thinking with others through his extensive writing and thereby had a profound influence on the character and direction of advertising growth.

Arch W. Shaw
1876-1962

21

Arch W. Shaw
1876-1962

by MELVIN T. COPELAND

A pioneer in proposing a systematic approach to the study of marketing, Arch W. Shaw began forty-five years ago to urge a replacement of rule-of-thumb procedures in marketing management by careful analysis, establishment of standards of performance, and thoughtful planning. At the same time he contemplated participation by university organizations and government agencies in that development.

Mr. Shaw was born in Jackson, Michigan, in 1876. After graduation from high school, he entered Olivet College but dropped out before completing the work for a degree. In 1899, at the age of 23, he joined with another young man, L.C. Walker, to found the Shaw-Walker Company, for the manufacture of office equipment. Four years later, while retaining his financial interest and a directorship in that company, he retired from active participation in its management and established the firm of A.W. Shaw Company, to publish the magazines *System* and *Factory*. The firm also published a sizeable list of books, chiefly on the elementary techniques of salesmanship and on various aspects of business management. That publishing business was sold to the McGraw-Hill Company in 1928.

Mr. Shaw always had a restless, inquisitive, and imaginative mind; and in 1910, in the midst of his successful career as a publisher, he decided to take a year off, to ascertain whether there was any thing of practical value to be found in academic cloisters. Consequently he went to Cambridge to attend classes in economics and to take a broad look around. There he became particularly interested in Professor Taussig's advanced course in economic theory, and Mr.

Journal of Marketing
Vol. XXII No. 3, January, 1958
Reprinted by Permission

Shaw's subsequent writing on the subject of marketing was substantially influenced by that course.

During that year in Cambridge, he also became acquainted with Edwin F. Gay, Professor of Economic History, who two years previously had been appointed Dean of the new Graduate School of Business Administration. From that acquaintance a life-long, intimate friendship between the two men developed. In 1911 Mr. Shaw was appointed Lecturer and Member of the Administrative Board at the Harvard Business School, on a part-time basis.

At the suggestion of Dean Gay, Mr. Shaw wrote an article which was published in the *Quarterly Journal of Economics*, August, 1912, and republished three years later with an introductory chapter, under the title *Some Problems in Market Distribution*. That was his most notable writing on the subject of marketing.

In his article Mr. Shaw classified distribution activities into those of demand creation and those of physical supply. He then proceeded to discuss various theoretical and operating aspects of those activities, and to stress their interdependence. Although a few books on salesmanship and advertising had been published before 1912, they were not of scholarly significance, and for students of marketing Mr. Shaw's article and book mark the beginning of the systematic literature in this field. His article provided the first broad discussion of the functions of marketing.

While Mr. Shaw sought in his article to establish an application of economic theory to marketing problems, his discussion, from a management point of view, of distribution policies of demand stimulation was particularly noteworthy. His concept of "the market contour" and his emphasis on the need for analysis of the market to determine that contour were far ahead of contemporary practice. And his criticism of the prevalent loose guesswork in the development of sales programs and advertising campaigns was strong. Although substantial progress has since been made in improving the handling of some of the problems that he discussed, a number of Mr. Shaw's observations are still pertinent today.

Out of the discussions between Mr. Shaw and Dean Gay in 1911, an idea emerged of setting up an organization to gather data on marketing costs and to establish standards of performance. Hence the Harvard Bureau of Business Research was founded, and Mr. Shaw made a financial contribution to enable the work to be gotten under way.

In his book on market distribution Mr. Shaw stated that, in his opinion, the federal government should undertake to collect, classify, and disseminate all the information available regarding the activities of business. Such an agency would cooperate, of course, with private institutions and trade associations. Prior to the publication of his book, he had advocated the same procedure through the editorial pages of *System*. The purpose of that proposal was to have the federal government set up a business service analogous to the field service of the Department of Agriculture for farmers.

Early in 1917, when the preparations for war were being stepped up rapidly, Mr. Shaw persuaded the Council of National Defense to approve the establishment of the Commercial Economy Board, of which he became chairman. The purpose of the Board was to effect economies in the use of labor and materials in civilian industry to aid in the war effort, and Mr. Shaw expected that the Board would function more or less in accordance with the plan which he previously had been advocating. While a study of retail delivery service was made, and while attention was given to some other analogous problems, the work of the Board actually was concentrated largely on the simplification of merchandise lines. When the War Industries Board was set up, the Commercial Economy Board became the Conservation Division, still under Mr. Shaw's chairmanship, of the W.I.B. The economies effected under that program proved to be very substantial.

Such were some of the undertakings pertaining to marketing to which Mr. Shaw applied his shrewd insight and fertile imagination.

Daniel Starch
1883-

22

Daniel Starch
1883-

by NEIL H. BORDEN

Few, if any men have had a greater influence on American advertising copy over the past three decades than has Daniel Starch. The Starch Advertisement Readership Service, often the subject of warm debate on grounds of the significance of readership and of research techniques employed, has had such wide distribution and has been used by so many advertising agencies and advertisers to guide their advertising copy techniques that few will gainsay the important role played by Dr. Starch in bringing about widespread adoption of copy research among advertisers.

Many agencies and advertisers over the years, in the conviction that readership measurements are significant, have carefully followed the Starch data to guide modification of their campaigns. Furthermore, many have carried on elaborate analyses of Starch data and therefrom have formulated generalizations to guide their copy practices. In turn, the debates on the meaning of readership and the techniques to be employed—often aimed at Starch, the leader—have in themselves been a stimulant to continuing experiments in copy research by both Starch and others. In business, research applied to copy has assumed important proportions. Truly, the influence of Daniel Starch has been great in the advertising segment of our economy. In recognition of this contribution, the American Marketing Association bestowed the Converse Award on him in 1953.

Dr. Starch, born some 73 years ago but still active in the research organization bearing his name, was among the pioneering psychologists who shortly after the turn of the century turned their atten-

Journal of Marketing
Vol. XXI No. 3, January, 1957
Reprinted by Permission

tion to the field of advertising. What was at first an academic interest in measuring the effects of advertising on human behavior in time became his chief interest in a business operation which by 1956 had come to employ some 160 people in the home office and an ever larger staff of field investigators directed by 10 full-time regional supervisors. The continuing collection of data on readership in magazines, newspapers, and business publications has been the chief effort of the organization over the past 25 years, but marketing and business research studies of many kinds have been produced by the Starch staff ever since its inception in 1919, a date which marks him as one of the earliest to establish a professional marketing research organization serving business. To dwell on the Starch readership studies would fail to give recognition to the many and varied contributions of Dr. Starch to the fields of psychology and business. Let us note some of the highlights of his long career.

Dr. Starch received his B.A. from Morningside College in 1903, his M.A. from the University of Iowa the following year, and his Ph.D. from Wisconsin in 1906. During the next fourteen years he taught psychology—a year at State University of Iowa, a year at Wellesley College, and twelve years at the University of Wisconsin. At the University of Wisconsin, Dr. Starch was an educational psychologist and while there produced a text in that field which went through several revisions. But early in his career he turned his attention increasingly to advertising. Teaching and research in the psychology of advertising began to replace educational psychology as his chief interest.

In our library I find a small volume by Starch on *Principles of Advertising—A Systematic Syllabus* published in 1910 by the University Cooperative Company of Madison. Thus, among the psychologists who early made advertising a major interest, Starch followed close behind Harlow Gale and Walter Dill Scott. In 1914 his *Advertising, Its Principles, Practice and Technique* appeared, which established him as a leader in the new field.

In the fall of 1920, as a result of his growing reputation in the psychology of advertising, he was invited to join the staff of the Harvard Business School. Here he was in charge of advertising instruction until 1926, when his growing interest in the application of psychology to business situations led him to leave the academic field in order to expand the activities of his own research organization and to direct the sizable program of research which the American Association of Advertising Agencies instituted in that year.

As a student in Professor Starch's classes in 1921-22 and as an instructor assisting him from 1924 to 1926, I came to know that behind his quiet, kindly reserve were determined drive, thoroughness, and steadfastness in carrying through any project or in seeking an answer to any problem that he tackled. During this period he gathered material for his monumental *Principles of Advertising*, published in 1923, which was for many years a leading text in the field.

It was at this time that Dr. Starch experimented with the recognition method as applied to published magazines which respondents had read in the normal course of their lives. Previously, the recognition method had been applied by Scott and Edward K. Strong to measurements of advertisements mounted in dummy copies which had been looked at or read within specified time limits under laboratory conditions. Approximately ten years later, in 1932, Starch started the continuing readership program with essentially the same techniques he had worked out in 1922. Convinced of the value of readership measurements by his analyses of a vast volume of data and by support from advertisers, Starch has carried on his program of continuous measurement.

Since leaving the academic ranks, an unusually large number of research projects have been carried out by Dr. Starch or under his direction. Many of these have been for clients not desirous of publication. But the published material is large and varied. Among the more important and better-known projects were the qualitative studies on newspaper and magazine circulation and the studies on duplication in circulation in these media, which he directed for the American Association of Advertising Agencies in the early 1930's. At this time he also published several volumes devoted to analyses of several million inquiries received from magazine and newspaper advertisements. Over the years also appeared studies made for individual publishers and broadcasting companies.

His interest in human behavior has extended beyond advertising and has resulted in publications on such varied subjects as socioeconomics, supported by data from his extensive research operations; on the development of executive ability; on "Faith, Fear and Fortunes"; and on analyses of retail trading areas. But Dr. Starch's biggest contribution has been in the field of advertising and his greatest influence has been in the area of copy research. It is in this area that he has issued a continuing series of pamphlets and articles over the years. It is the area in which he still labors with the objective of developing additional measurement techniques of help in evaluating the effects of advertising.

Editors' Afternote: In April 1973, Dr. Starch submitted the following paragraphs for inclusion in this volume:

Since Professor Neil H. Borden wrote the piece about me in the 1957 series on Biographies of Marketing Men, I have continued to be busy in the general area of marketing research. My chief activities have been centered around measuring the correlation between the perception of advertising messages and the current use and purchase of the brand or product advertised.

These studies appeared in a number of articles in various journals and were fully summarized in my book *Measuring Advertising Readership and Results*, McGraw-Hill, 1966.

I continued to be busy. A book entitled *Look Ahead to Life* (Vantage Press, New York) has just come out. I am presently working on a book about Great Books.

Harry R. Tosdal
1889-

23

Harry R. Tosdal
1889-

by ROSS M. CUNNINGHAM

DR. HARRY R. TOSDAL has pioneered in developing the area of sales management, and personifies this field to the many students and business executives who have known him and his work. His concept of sales management has been consistently broad, embracing product planning, distribution and pricing policy, development of selling and advertising programs, organization and management of salesmen, and control of sales operations. This is essentially the range of activities included in the "marketing manager" concept which is now attracting widespread attention.

As was true of some other early workers in marketing, his academic training and initial interest was in economics. With an S.B. degree from St. Olaf College, Minnesota, in 1909 (Hon. LL.D., 1940), he received his Ph.D. in Economics from Harvard in 1915 after study abroad at the Universities of Leipzig and Berlin. Cartels in the German iron and potash industries were the subject of his doctoral dissertation, and articles on this topic as well as price maintenance and open-price associations appeared in the *Quarterly Journal of Economics* and *American Economic Review* between 1914 and 1919.

Dr. Tosdal taught for a year in the Economics Department at Massachusetts Institute of Technology, and then at Boston University for three years, during which time he became head of the Economics Department. He joined the staff of the Harvard Business School in 1920 as Assistant Professor and Director of Student Research, and was appointed Professor of Marketing in 1922. After becoming Professor Emeritus in 1956 he taught another year at Harvard before retiring.

Journal of Marketing
Vol. XXIII No. 1, July, 1958
Reprinted by Permission

In developing the field of sales management Dr. Tosdal published *Problems in Sales Management* in 1921, which was revised several times in subsequent years. This was followed in 1922 by a case book on problems in export sales management. Although he did no further writing in the export field, it was one of continuing interest to him. A third book, *Principles of Personal Selling*, published in 1925, was the first scholarly effort to seek out and describe principles involved in personal salesmanship and the management of salesmen. The first edition of *Introduction to Sales Management*, a combination of text and cases, appeared in 1933, and the most recent edition in 1957.

One of Dr. Tosdal's particular interests is that of compensation plans for salesmen. This interest led to an intensive study of compensation plans, published in two volumes in 1953 by the Harvard University Division of Research.

Another interest relates to the study of consumer demand and its application to the marketing problems of the firm. An analysis of consumer demand appeared in 1938 as a chapter in *Business and Modern Society*, as well as articles on the topic in the *Harvard Business Review* and *The Journal of Marketing* in the following year.

Perhaps his keenest interest, however, relates to the widespread lack of understanding of the contribution made by the selling function to our economic system. He feels that this lack of understanding is in large measure responsible for the critical attitudes toward selling and marketing in general. These attitudes, in turn, discourage young people from entering selling and advertising as a career, and deny to many of those working in the field the fullest measure of emotional satisfaction with their contribution. His deep-seated desire to improve this situation resulted in the publication last year of a book entitled *Selling in Our Economy—An Economic and Scoial Analysis of Selling and Advertising.*

Other publications include a section in *Case Method of Instruction*, edited by Cecil Fraser in 1931; chapters in *Marketing by Manufacturers*, edited by C.F. Phillips in 1946; *What Salesmen Think of Sales Managers* (with Ross M. Cunningham), Boston Sales Managers Club, 1940; and many articles in various professional journals.

Dr. Tosdal has always·been very active in editorial work. He was chairman of the Faculty Committee at the Harvard Business School which recommended the initiation of the *Harvard Business Review* in 1922, and was its faculty editor from that time through the year

1939. He was also on the editorial board of *The Journal of Marketing* from 1937 to 1939. He has an unusually comprehensive and intimate knowledge of existing literature, not only in marketing but in many other areas related to marketing.

In the field of executive development he taught advanced-management courses at the Harvard Business School for mature executives from 1928 to 1937, and from 1944 to 1957. In 1955 he participated in an advanced-management course in Hawaii for business executives drawn from the mainland islands, Australia, and the Far East, and was in charge of this program in 1956. During the current year he is participating in the first year of a new school in Switzerland for experienced business executives, known as Imede (Institue pour l'Etude des Methodes de l'Entreprise). This school in Lausanne has an affiliation with the University of Lausanne.

Among his business activities, he is Chairman of the Board of Directors of a wholesale appliance distributor, and has been a consultant to such companies as General Electric, Remington Rand, Gulf Oil, and Whiting Corporation. He was a Director of the Publix Shirt Company from 1944 to 1952.

In the professional-association field, Dr. Tosdal was President of the National Association of Marketing Teachers in 1935, and later was a Director of the American Marketing Association. Throughout his career he has been very active in the National Sales Executives Association and particularly the Boston club. He was President of the Boston Sales Managers Club from 1932 to 1934.

Dr. Tosdal has an orderly and analytical approach to the complex problems of marketing, coupled with an unusual understanding of the human problems in business organizations. His dry sense of humor enlivens many a classroom session and conference with faculty and business associates. His insistence on defining "the job to be done" has helped many to clarify their thinking on the inevitably complicated topic of suitable organization structures for marketing operations. He has always been active in faculty affairs at the Harvard Business School, and is widely respected by his colleagues for his effectiveness in the many educational programs developed at the school

Those who have had the good fortune to be closely associated with him, as was the author for his first four working years as research assistant and instructor, know of his deep interest in encouraging and assisting the development of younger people.

Editors' Afternote: The editors were unable to learn of Professor Tosdal's activities since 1958.

Roland Snow Vaile
1889-1970

24

Roland Snow Vaile
1889-1970

by E.T. GRETHER

When Roland S. Vaile retired at the end of the academic year 1954-55, the University of Minnesota lost one of its great teachers, authors, faculty statesmen, and scholars. Roland Vaile's active, inquiring mind and scholarly interests could not be narrowly confined within the field of marketing. In his teaching, research, and writings, he touched an extraordinary variety of problems and facets of marketing in addition to other areas of knowledge. He has had the thrill of being a pioneer and innovator as well as attempting a better integration between fact and theory. These characteristics showed themselves early in his career in his work in the field of orchard management at the Citrus Experiment Station in Southern California. His 1924 study of orchard practices in the citrus industry was considered one of the best farm management studies of that period. He was one of the first to use multiple correlation procedures in this field. His 1927 paper on the long-term effects of cooperative marketing used a particularly interesting approach to the analysis of the diffusion of benefits from cooperative marketing.

Perhaps the leading example of his ability in innovation was his *Economics of Advertising*, published in 1927. This volume, so he stated, stemmed from his years of experience with the sales problems of the California citrus industry together with the inquisitive insistence of his students. Prior to Roland Vaile's study, the discussions of the significance of advertising were either highly partisan or fragmentary and incidental. Vaile's volume displayed the combination of theoretical and empirical analysis that has been characteristic of all of his work.

Journal of Marketing
Vol. XX No. 4, April, 1956
Reprinted by Permission

During some 30 years Roland Vaile ranged over many of the important aspects and problems of marketing in the classroom and in his writings. Our library in Berkeley, for example, contains 20 books, monographs, and special studies under his name alone or in collaboration. Thirty-four other papers in academic journals and similar publications are known to this writer. On several occasions, also, he has acted as editor of volumes and research series. From April 1937 until the spring of 1941, he was the editor of *The Journal of Marketing*. His influence was very important in the development of *The Journal*.

In addition to the topics already mentioned, his prolific pen has contributed to the analysis of the marketing of several commodities, including citrus fruits, grocery products, coal, grain, flour, and gasoline. He produced also a number of noteworthy functional studies dealing with storage and warehousing, transportation, advertising and selling. He investigated and reported on various aspects of marketing organization, including agricultural and consumers cooperatives, retailing, wholesaling, and the organized commodity exchanges. He participated in or directed the investigation of a number of broad, interesting, local community studies in Minnesota, especially of Red Wing. The focus of attention in the Red Wing study was the impact of war and peace on community problems and organization. He concerned himself often with currently important national issues such as the impact of the depression on modes of consumption, the economic effects of the National Industrial Recovery Administration, economic planning, govermental economic controls, and antitrust problems and policies. He visited portions of Asia and for years taught a course dealing with the economic systems of Asia, and published an important paper dealing with Southeast Asia. He always had a major interest in the field of income and consumption in which he has long been a well-recognized authority. His 1938 and 1951 books on income and consumption in collaboration with Helen C. Canoyer gave him a high position in this significant area of economic and marketing analysis.

For years he has participated in the discussions and endeavors to develop a better "theory" or framework for the study of marketing. Although he has ranged widely, his basic orientation was from economic analysis. He contended that marketing still had a long way to go in utilizing the available theoretical economic apparatus. Even in his work in the field of consumption, where he drew upon other social sciences, he held that the basic issues for marketing are clustered around those of economic rationality. Perhaps this outlook stemmed from his initial work in the field of agricultural economics. This same orientation showed itself in his collaborative endeavor (published in 1952) to interpret the role and functioning of marketing in the American economy. He was much more concerned with the economic and social effects of marketing than in its business aspects in the business and managerial aspects of marketing.

The literature of marketing will long bear the imprint of Roland Vaile, both in its general character and in the examination of specific products, areas, institutions, and problems. In the words of a contemporary scholar at another university, "When future students of marketing attempt to trace back into the past concepts with which they are dealing, almost regardless of the topic they are studying, they are likely to discover that Professor Vaile has been there before them. They will find his observations original and realistic, his suggestions challenging, and his conclusions filled with an authentic wisdom which few of his contemporaries have equalled."

Yet, Roland Vaile is probably an even greater teacher than writer. According to one of his former colleagues, "His graduate students appreciated his careful and intelligent advice; his capacity to open up new areas for exploration by those students interested and willing to investigate them; his "steel trap" mind combined with patience and understanding of the slower thinkers; his interest in earnest and sincere students and his willingness to spend unlimited time and energy to help students. . .His unusual ability to translate the theoretical into practical have been valued by all of his students. He brought to the solution of a problem great insight, excellent judgment and quick evaluation of the critical factors involved."

Finally, it should be noted that Roland S. Vaile was an active leader of the faculty of the University of Minnesota in general and in the School of Business Administration in particular. The integrity and high standards and breadth of interests that characterized his teachings and research brought to him high responsibilities and opportunities in faculty government.

Editors' Afternote: Professor E. Alan Hale, of the California State University, Sàn Diego, furnished the following paragraphs for use in this volume:

Roland Vaile taught at this university (formerly San Diego State College) from August 31, 1956 to July 1, 1960, during a period when its Marketing program was in its early stage of development. He regularly taught a seminar class in Marketing. I sat in on his course one semester to observe his style. It was low key but very effective. He would begin a topic in a lecture by saying, "Let's see if any part of this subject catches fire." After a few minutes, students would begin to ask questions and discuss the subject.

Professor Vaile appeared to run his class with a very loose rein, but the class nearly always stayed on the topic. He was a very valued member of the department here, and helped immeasurably in our planning and long-range development.

[Professor Vaile died on June 3, 1970]

Louis D.H. Weld
1882-1946

25

Louis D.H. Weld
1882-1946

by DONALD R.G. COWAN

The training of the academic scholar and the realism of the practical business man combined in "Doc" Weld to make him one of the most prolific of the early contributors to marketing knowledge.

After a year at Harvard, he transferred to Bowdoin College and was prominent there in the Debating, Junior Economics, and Glee Clubs, and the varsity track and relay teams. He was elected to Phi Beta Kappa and graduated *summa cum laude* in 1905. He obtained his M.A. in economics at the University of Illinois in 1907, and his Ph.D. at Columbia University in 1908. Few people who knew Dr. Weld in his subsequent business career were acquainted with his teaching experience in economics and the opportunities it afforded him to pioneer in studies of marketing. Following a brief service with the International Banking Company in London, he served as Instructor in Economics at the University of Washington 1908-09 and at the Wharton School of Commerce and Finance, the University of Pennsylvania 1909-10. After nearly two years as a Special Agent of the U.S. Bureau of the Census, he became Assistant Professor of Economics at the University of Minnesota 1912-16, and at age 33 Professor of Business Administration in the Sheffield Scientific School, Yale University 1916-17.

While at Minnesota, he was shifted in 1913 from the Economics Department on the main campus to the College of Agriculture. The College wanted to develop a knowledge of how Minnesota products were marketed, and fortunately required Dr. Weld to spend most of his time in research work. Describing this early experience, he said; "When I began to teach marketing in the fall of 1913, there was

Journal of Marketing
Vol. XXV No. 2, October, 1960
Reprinted by Permission

practically no literature on the subject. I had to go out and dig up my own information."

He studied at first hand the movement of grain, the use of future trading, the shipping of butter and eggs from country producers to city consumers, the activities of the cooperative shipping associations, the central exchanges and the auctions, and, in addition, the methods of price determination at succeeding stages in the marketing channels. "As a result I was able not only to give my students firsthand information that had never before been collected, but at the same time to develop in my own mind some general principles about marketing, including the functions of middlemen, the factors affecting the cost of marketing, etc." He was called before a special committee of the Minnesota legislature to explain why he taught his "dangerous doctrines" about the efficiency of marketing and future trading.

At the annual meeting of the American Economic Association in December, 1914, Weld read a significant paper on "Market Distribution," apparently the first comprehensive presentation to that Association of marketing as it is today. In it he took economists to task for their general neglect of this subject. "Marketing is a part of production. It has to do with the creation of time, place and possession utilities, whereas manufacturing has to do with the creation of form utilities. In discussing the problems of production, economists have usually had in mind primarily the manufacturing end, and they have drawn their illustrations of division of labor, large-scale production, organization of industry, etc., from this field . . .And yet that part of production . . .covered by marketing is extremely important as . . .a comparison of factory or farm cost with the final retail price of almost any commodity will prove . . . Economists agree that they have neglected this branch of their subject, but few realize either the alluring fields for research which offer themselves, or the serious consequences that their neglect has brought about."

At the Association's annual meetings in 1918 and suceeding years, Weld served as chairman of informal round tables on the teaching of marketing, and, with a handful of kindred spirits, laid the foundation for the subsequent formal organization of the teachers and practitioners, now the American Marketing Association.

Meanwhile Weld wrote several Minnesota Social Science bulletins describing his marketing studies, and in 1916 published his important book *The Marketing of Farm Products.* It became the pioneer text in new marketing courses, and the reading of it was required of this biographer at Queen's University in 1917. Articles by him were published on "Marketing Functions and Mercantile Organizations" in the *American Economic Review* (June, 1917), and on "Marketing Agencies Between Manufacturer and Whole-sales" in the *Quarterly Journal of Economics* (August, 1917).

In August, 1917, "Doc" Weld was engaged by Swift and Company, leading marketer of livestock, meat, and related products both nationally and internationally. He was assigned a two-fold task—to help in preparing the company's defense in the Federal Trade Commission's investigation of the meat packing industry, and to present to the public a clear picture of the competitive marketing services rendered by the Company. He was the packers' first spokes-man to clarify the competitive forces determining the prices of livestock and meat, the public's benefit from the industry's important distribution services, the lure of profits in promoting marketing efficiency resulting in lower prices for consumers, and the small profit-reward amounting to "a fraction of a cent per pound" earned by the more efficient marketers.

In the widely-read Swift yearbooks he told in simple narrative the economic story of that business. His lucid style and direct ex-pression created a great demand for him as a writer and a speaker. Some of his papers were "The Economics of Advertising" (*Printers' Ink*, July 11, 1918), "Do Principles of Large Scale Production Apply to Merchandising?" (Proceedings of the Thirty Fifth Annual Meeting, American Economic Association, March 1923), "The Value of Cost Analysis" (Ninth Annual Convention, Automotive Equipment Association, November 13, 1924). These articles and his collaboration with Fred E. Clark in writing the book *Marketing Agricultural Products in the United States* (1932) marked the final eclipse of Weld's waning interest in general marketing principles, functions and costs.

For Weld, the economics of marketing was a living thing, a basis for sound decision and prompt action in practical affairs, rather than a mere collection of academic abstractions. He firmly believed that free competition, if allowed to operate, would automatically establish equilibrium prices and regulate the flow of goods as be-tween different uses, places, and periods of time. In discussing lead-ing papers by Irving Fisher and B.M. Anderson at the annual meet-ing of the American Economic Association in December, 1917, Weld expresses with characteristic temerity his concern at econo-mists' lost opportunities:

". . .The trouble with economists is that they do not get near enough to present-day, practical problems. After the war, they may be able to tell, in an uninteresting way, why price control was a success or failure; but they are powerless and lacking in sufficient influence to help solve such a problem when it is forced upon the country.

"I am not denouncing theoretical economics by any means; I merely appeal for a linking up of theory with practical everyday problems. This calls for more contact with business machinery and business men. More valuable contributions can be made to the theory of market price by getting out into the markets with a market reporter than by cogitation in a closet. Let us try to get away from the reputation of being "theoretical" and develop a reputation for being able to put our theories to some practical use." (*American Economic Review* Vol. 8, No. 1 Supp., March, 1918, pp. 226-267).

With such strong convictions, Weld soon persuaded the officers of Swift and Company that a Commercial Research Department could help in solving the company's management problems. It was established in 1917, probably the first in a leading manufacturing concern. In becoming its first manager, Weld saw to it that he reported to the president.

As department heads increasingly submitted their analysis and recommendations, he became more and more engrossed in the possibilities of increasing profits through studies of forecasting raw-material supplies and finished product sales, inventory control, price determination, salesmen's potentials, incentives and performance, product branding and preference, advertising themes and media, and company relations with livestock suppliers, employees, and the consuming public. He wrote about "The Progress of Commercial Research" (*Harvard Business Review*, January, 1923), and "The Economist as an Aid to Management" (American Management Association, Annual Convention Series No. 16, 1925). He encouraged his assistants to use statistical analysis and measurement problems. He stimulated their imagination, supported their initiative, and proudly recognized their contributions. It was a rich experience to be one of his team.

Weld's interest in marketing management and manipulation became so great that in 1926 he accepted the invitation of his Bowdoin fraternity brother, H.K. McCann, to become an account executive in McCann's advertising agency in New York. Later he became Director of Research of the McCann-Erickson Agency, filling that post for the remainder of his life. From 1927 onward, semi-popular

articles on market management flowed from his pen into *Printers'
Ink* and other executive-read publications on such subjects as
Measuring Sales Potentials, the Quality of Magazine Circulation,
The Market for an Individual Commodity, Retail Sales as a Measure
of Buying Power, and Putting Science into Advertising. In more
technical publications, some of his papers were: "Use of Correlation
in the Measurement of Sales Potentials" (*Journal of the American
Statistical Association*, Vol. 27, Supp., March, 1932), "Manufactur-
ers' Advertising and Sales Promotion Policies" (American Manage-
ment Association, Consumers' Marketing Series, No. 12, 1933),
"The Problem of Measuring Radio Coverage" (*Journal of the
American Statistical Association*, Vol. 33, March 1938), "The Place
of Marketing Research During a National Emergency" (*Journal of
Marketing*, Vol. 4 April, 1940) and "Early Experience in Teaching
Courses in Marketing" (*Journal of Marketing*, Vol. 5, April, 1941).

His later contributions were not confined to writing. He developed and put to wide practical use the *McCann Index of General
Buying Power by Areas* (The H.K. McCann Company, New York,
1930). *Printers' Ink* induced him in 1935 to compile and publish
estimates of the annual expenditures for advertising in newspaper,
magazine, radio, outdoor and farm paper media, thereby providing
for the first barometer of the changes in advertising volume. His
estimates were later adopted by the U.S. Department of Commerce
Monthly Survey of Current Business. The Advertising Research
Foundation appointed him to counsel with Neil H. Borden in the
latter's monumental study , *The Economic Effects of Advertising*,
published in 1942.

Weld was President of New York's Market Research Council in
1931 and of the American Marketing Society in 1933. He took an
active part in the Cooperative Analysis of Broadcasting, the research
work of the American Association of Advertising Agencies, and the
meetings of the American Marketing Association. In 1946 he died
at his summer home in Gloucester, Massachusetts. In 1949 the
American Marketing Association awarded him, posthumously, the
Paul D. Converse Award for Outstanding Contributions to Science
in Marketing.

Selected Bibliography
For Further Reading

List A - materials directly related to the thrust of the "Pioneers in Marketing" book.

Books:

Bartels, Robert. *The Development of Marketing Thought*, Richard D. Irwin, Inc., Homewood, Ill.: 1962, Appendix A particularly.

_____. *Marketing Theory and Metatheory*, Richard D. Irwin, Inc., Homewood, Ill.: 1970.

Converse, P. D. *The Beginnings of Marketing Thought in the United States, with Reminiscence of Some of the Pioneer Scholars.* Bureau of Business Research Studies in Marketing, No. 3, Austin: University of Texas, 1959.

Coolsen, Frank G. *Marketing Thought in the United States in the Late Nineteeth Century*, Lubbock, Texas: Texas Tech Press, 1960.

Articles:

Maynard, H. H. "Early Teachers of Marketing," *Journal of Marketing*, VII (October, 1942), p. 158.

Litman, Simon. "The Beginnings of Teaching Marketing in American Universities," *Journal of Marketing*, XV (October, 1950), p. 220.

List B - materials more related to marketing theory but which have some relevance to the subject matter of this volume.

Books:

Fisk, George, *New Essays in Marketing Theory*, Boston, Mass.: Allyn and Bacon, 1971.

Halbert, Michael. *The Meaning and Sources of Marketing Theory*, New York: McGraw-Hill Book Co., 1965.

Howard, John. *Marketing Theory*, Boston, Mass.: Allyn and Bacon, 1965.

Kernan, Jerome B., and Montrose S. Sommers, ed., *Perspectives in Marketing Theory*, New York: Appleton-Century-Crofts, 1968.

Schwartz, George. *Development of Marketing Theory*, Cincinnati, Ohio: South-Western Publishing Company, 1963.

Sequential Order Of Articles That Appeared In The
Journal Of Marketing

Roland Snow Vaile
   by E. T. Grether

Journal of Marketing
Vol. XX No. 4 April, 1956

Charles Coolidge Parlin
   by Wroe Alderson

Journal of Marketing
Vol. XXI No. 4 July, 1956

Paul Terry Cherington
   by Archibald M. Crossley

Journal of Marketing
Vol. XXI No. 2 Oct., 1956

Daniel Starch
   by Neil H. Borden

Journal of Marketing
Vol. XXI No. 3 Jan., 1957

Paul Henry Nystrom
   by Delbert J. Duncan

Journal of Marketing
similar article by
Delbert J. Duncan
Vol. XXI No. 4 April, 1957

Fred Emerson Clark
   by R. M. Clewett

Journal of Marketing
Vol. XXII No. 1 July, 1957

Melvin T. Copeland
   by Malcolm P. McNair

Journal of Marketing
Vol. XXII No. 2 Oct.,1957

Arch W. Shaw
   by Melvin T. Copeland

Journal of Marketing
Vol. XXII No. 3 Jan., 1958

Edwin Griswold Nourse
   by E. T. Grether

Journal of Marketing
Vol. XXII No. 4 April, 1958

Harry R. Tosdal
   by Ross M. Cunningham

Journal of Marketing
Vol. XXIII No. 1 April, 1958

Paul Dulaney Converse
   by Harvey W. Huegy

Journal of Marketing
Vol. XXIII No. 2 Oct., 1958

Edward A. Filene
Lincoln Filene
   by Daniel Bloomfield

Journal of Marketing
Vol. XXIII No. 3 Jan., 1959

Harold H. Maynard
  by Theodore N. Beckman

Journal of Marketing
Vol. XXIII No. 4 April, 1959

Leverett Samuel Lyon
  by N. H. Engle

Journal of Marketing
Vol. XXIV No. 1 July, 1959

Benjamin Horace Hibbard
  by Henry E. Erdman

Journal of Marketing
Vol. XXIV No. 2 Oct., 1959

Hugh Elmer Agnew
  by William J. McKeon

Journal of Marketing
Vol. XXIV No 3 Jan., 1960

Henry E. Erdman
  by George L. Mehren

Journal of Marketing
Vol. XXIV No 4 April, 1960

Norris Arthur Brisco
  by John W. Wingate

Journal of Marketing
Vol. XXV No. 1 July, 1960

Louis D. H. Weld
  by Donald R. G. Cowan

Journal of Marketing
Vol. XXV No. 2 Oct., 1960

George Burton Hotchkiss
  by D. B. Lucas

Journal of Marketing
Vol. XXV No. 3 Jan., 1961

Ralph Starr Butler
  by J. H. Westing

Journal of Marketing
similar article by
James Playsted Wood
Vol. XXV No. 4 April, 1961

Walter Dill Scott
  by C. H. Sandage

Journal of Marketing
Vol. XXV No. 5 July, 1961

Stanley B. Resor
  by Laurence Wile Jacobs

Journal of Marketing
similar article by
James Playsted Wood
Vol. XXV No. 6 Oct., 1961

21527

Wright, John Sherman

Pioneers in Marketing

† 24608